JESUS IS THE HEALER

TERRY KINARD

PUBLISHED by PARABLES
Earthly Stories with a Heavenly Meaning

Jesus Is The Healer
Terry Kinard

Published By Parables
November, 2018

All Rights Reserved. No part of this book may be reproduced or utilized in any form or by any means, electronic or mechanical, including photocopying, recording, or by any information storage and retrieval system, without permission in writing from the author.

    ISBN 978-1-945698-75-0
    Printed in the United States of America

Readers should be aware that Internet Web sites offered as citations and/or sources for further information may have been changed or disappeared between the time this was written and the time it is read.

JESUS IS THE HEALER

TERRY KINARD

PUBLISHED by PARABLES
Earthly Stories with a Heavenly Meaning

CONTENTS

1. Why is Sickness in the World? — 3
2. Dealing with Sin and Sickness — 19
3. Biblical Basis for Divine Healing — 25
4. Healing is a Temporal Blessing — 37
5. Healing is a Covenant Promise — 45
6. Man Healed of Palsy — 49
7. Mt. Ebal and Mt. Gerizim — 53
8. The Woman at the Well — 57
9. Has Jesus Changed? — 63
10. Who Can Receive from God? — 75
11. Why Are Some Not Healed? — 83
12. Faith is the Key to Healing — 87
13. How to Receive Healing — 99
14. Guidelines to Receive Healing — 105
15. Healing Scriptures — 111

Acknowledgements

Many circumstances, sermons, writings, testimonies, and individuals contributed to the writing of this book. Most of all, the Lord Jesus guided me into truth through His precious Holy Spirit, and brought me to the present level of understanding.

I am thankful to many giants of the faith, including some unsung spiritual fathers, especially Pastor Buddy and Pat Turner of Fairfield Christian Center in Fairfield, Texas. Much of the material for this book comes from teachings I have received through Pastor Buddy over many years. His insights from God's Word have built my faith, and enabled me to walk in divine health for the past thirty years.

Other ministers who have spoken volumes into my life include: Oscar and Linda Roan, Pastor Eugene and Nancy Green, Pastor Kent and Mary Merrill, Pastor Billy and Thelma Grate, Pastor Charles York, John and Marcia Kendall, Tracy Yates, Jimmy and Cindy Seay, Barbara Cooper, Judy Hester, and a host of more recent friends and fellow laborers in the Lord, including Pastor Scott and Jennifer Smith, Pastor David and Carolyn Combest, and Pastor Jon and Toni Ogle.

Finally, I wish to thank my husband Mike, daughter Brooke, my mother, Betty Culberhouse, and my assistant and dear friend, Marcia Munson. They put up with many hours of my being absent, to make this book come together. Their grace, patience and understanding has been greatly appreciated.

To all these I dedicate this book. My prayer is that it may benefit the Kingdom of God, to help God's people grasp the reality of His precious promises for healing in this life. My hope and desire is that we all may come into a greater knowledge of His will, and live physically and spiritually healthy and strong, and enjoy all His good treasure.

Most of all, I thank the Lord for His mercy and grace, and the experiences that caused me to reach out for His healing touch, and enabled me to walk in divine health.

Terry Kinard

1

WHY IS SICKNESS IN THE WORLD?

Disease and pain are very real. No one who has ever spent a sleepless night, tossing with fever or aches and pains, could deny it. Neither could one who has sat by the hospital bed of someone they love, ever doubt that sickness is a very real fact of life, nor could they deny that we are very limited in our human strength to defeat this enemy. Although God created man in His own image, originally without physical susceptibility to sickness, <u>the entrance of sin through temptation opened the door to disease</u>. Sin and sickness both passed upon the entire human race through Adam's disobedience and defiled God's original good world.

God Created a "Good" World
And Gave Man Dominion

1. God created this world a paradise.

"In the beginning, God created the heaven and the earth" (Genesis 1:1). God created everything: Day and Night, the heavens, dry land, seas, plants, trees, the sun, moon, stars, planets, sea creatures, land creatures, birds, and finally, man himself. "And God saw every thing that He had made, and behold, it was <u>very good</u>" (Genesis 3:31).

2. God created man in His own image, both male and female, and gave him dominion (power) over the earth. It's an interesting fact that "...God blessed them, and called their name Adam" (Genesis 5:2). Women have the same spiritual dominion as men over the earth.

"And God said, Let us make man in our <u>image</u> (phantom, illusion, resemblance), after our <u>likeness</u> (model, shape). So God created man in his own image, in the image of God created he him; male and female created He them" (Genesis 3:26-27).

"And God blessed them, and God said unto them, Be fruitful, and multiply, and replenish the earth, and subdue it: and *<u>have dominion</u>*...over every living thing that moveth upon the earth" (Genesis 1:28).

"...the earth hath he given to the children of men" (Psalm 115:16).

God placed the man and woman He created in the midst of the garden of Eden to take care of it and to enjoy it. God created the man, and then the woman, not only to have relationship with each other, populate the world, and enjoy the blessings of all of Creation, but also to have fellowship with Him, their Creator.

3. God loves mankind that He created.

He came down and walked with man in the cool of the evening, (Genesis 3:8) communing with him. God gave man dominion over the entire earth and every living thing in it (Genesis 1:28) and then gave man the opportunity to live forever by eating of the Tree of Life (Genesis 2:9).*

*Why Not the Tree of Life?

God commanded Adam and Eve not to eat the fruit of the Tree of the knowledge of Good and Evil. "And the LORD God commanded the man, saying, Of every tree of the garden thou mayest freely eat: But of the tree of the knowledge of good and evil, thou shalt not eat of it: for in the day that thou eatest thereof thou shalt surely die" (Genesis 2:16-17).

*It is curious to me that God gave no command to them concerning the Tree of Life. All they had to do to live forever was to eat its fruit! I wonder if it was unpleasant to the eye, not something that would draw their attention naturally. Perhaps the fruit was unappealing, or had no pleasant fragrance. Or perhaps, because it was in the middle of the garden, it was not very accessible. It wasn't in the main stream of their common path.

It is interesting to consider, however, that it WAS available to them, and they ignored it. Maybe they were so enjoying living on the outer edges, the fringes of God's blessing, that they had no occasion to press into the thick growth of the center of the garden, and by not pressing in, somehow "missed" the Tree of Life…

"Enter ye in at the strait gate: for wide is the gate, and broad is the way, that leadeth to destruction, and many there be which go in thereat: because strait is the gate, and narrow is the way, which leadeth unto life, and <u>few there be that find it</u>" (Matthew 7:14).

Have you ever found what you were not looking for? Maybe. You may stumble unexpectedly across something occasionally, but as the old farmers used to say, "Even a blind hog finds an acorn once in a while." Generally, though, we find what we look for. Have you missed the Tree of Life in the midst of God's creation, because you've been living too close to the edge? The old song says, "The Way of the Cross Leads Home." God reaches out to us, saying, "And ye shall seek me, and find me, when ye shall search for me with all your heart" (Jeremiah 29:13).

It is also curious that the serpent drew Eve's attention to the Tree of the Knowledge of Good and Evil, and NOT to the Tree of Life. (Satan wanted to control Adam and Eve, and interrupt their relationship with God through disobedience. Satan wanted them serving him, not God. And he has not changed! He tells us lies about God too, hoping we, like Eve, will fall into his deceptive trap!)

Evidently Eve had lived some length of time in the Garden of Eden without having been too much aware of either tree, that is, until the serpent began his marketing job on her (Genesis 3:1-6). Oh, yes, Satan definitely tries to sell his lies, packaged in flattery and twisted facts! Verse six says "...when the woman saw..."

Had she never noticed before? And is it possible, that she missed the Tree of Life growing near the Tree of Knowledge of Good and Evil?

Consider how different history would have been, had Adam and Eve eaten of the Tree of Life instead of the Tree of Knowledge of Good and Evil. They would have lived forever in fellowship with God, and received His blessings, and life would have passed to all men rather than death! By eating of the Tree of Life, they would have avoided the punishment and curse of sin. The dominion they had enjoyed would have continued uninterrupted and unthreatened. All they put their hands to would have prospered. They would have remained in the presence and fellowship of the Lord, and enjoyed peace and happiness. Sin would never have entered the world, and there would be no sickness or disease. And there would have been no need for Jesus to come and suffer and die for us. Oh, that Adam and Eve had acted differently!

But wait! There is still hope! Because in spite of their disobedience, God still loved them, and sent His Son to redeem, or buy us back from the lawful penalty and curse of sin!

He took our penalty, our punishment, by giving His life on Calvary, and by that sacrifice, He lifted the curse of the law from us, appeased the justice of God Almighty, and restored to us the blessings of fellowship, provision, and eternal life that he offered Adam and Eve in the Garden.

"Christ hath redeemed us from the curse of the law, being made a curse for us: for it is written, Cursed is every one that hangs on a tree (dies on a cross of crucifixion): That the blessing of Abraham might come on the Gentiles through Jesus Christ; that we might receive the promise of the Spirit through faith" (Galatians 3:13-14).

God's holiness, his justice, has been appeased (satisfied) by Jesus' death on the cross of Calvary. God is no longer angry with man. We are reconciled, restored, to the fellowship that Adam had before he disobeyed in the garden of Eden.

"God was in Christ, reconciling the world unto himself, not imputing their trespasses unto them…" (II Corinthians 5:19).

We can eat of the Tree of Life now, by faith, and become a branch, drawing from the life source of God. "I am the vine, ye are the branches: He that abideth in me, and I in him, the same bringeth forth much fruit: for without me ye can do nothing" (John 15:5).

Man Has Free Will

4. Man was created with free will, and therefore, had the choice whether or not to obey God's one command.

"The Lord God commanded the man, saying, Of every tree of the garden thou mayest freely eat: But of the tree of the knowledge of good and evil, thou shalt not eat of it: for in the day that thou eatest thereof thou shalt surely die" (Genesis 2:16-17).

5. Adam made the wrong choice. (Genesis 3:1-7) He chose to rebel and disobey God's command, and sin entered the world for the first time.

"She (Eve) took of the fruit thereof, and did eat, and gave also unto her husband with her; and he did eat. And the eyes of them both were opened, and they knew that they were naked...And Adam and his wife hid themselves from the presence of the Lord God...And he (God) said, Who told thee that thou wast naked? Hast thou eaten of the tree, whereof I commanded thee that thou shouldest not eat?" (Genesis 3:4-6).

Technically, it was Eve who listened to the serpent, ate of the fruit, and gave it to her husband to eat. But since God had commanded Adam personally, and he stood as the head of the home, his was the greater sin of disobedience, while Eve's was a sin of deception. "For the husband is the head of the wife, even as Christ is the head of the church: and he is the savior of the body. Therefore as the church is subject unto Christ, so let the wives be to their own husbands in everything. Husbands, love your wives, even as Christ also loved the church, and gave himself for it" (Ephesians 5:23-25).

When husbands love and make sacrifices for their wives as Christ sacrificed for the Church, then wives can easily submit to that leadership of love. But rules without relationship bring rebellion.

Disobedience Brought the Curse
With Death and Disease

6. Man's disobedience to God brought a curse on the earth. The curse includes sickness and death. (Genesis 3:14-19)

God punished Adam, Eve, and the serpent, and then sent His angel to drive man from the Garden of Eden. The ground was cursed, and no longer brought forth abundant fruit without backbreaking toil. Thorns and thistles appeared, which had not existed previously. For her disobedience and rebellion, the woman was cursed to bring forth children in sorrow and pain, and be ruled over by her husband; and worst of all, death passed upon mankind. From this point on, man's days would be numbered, and he would experience physical death and disease that leads to death.

"And unto Adam God said, Because thou hast hearkened (listened) unto the voice of thy wife, and hast eaten of the tree, of which I commanded thee, saying, Thou shalt not eat of it: cursed is the ground for thy sake; in sorrow shalt thou eat of it all the days of thy life; thorns and thistles shall it bring forth to thee; and thou shalt eat the herb of the field; In the sweat of thy face shalt thou eat bread, till thou return unto the ground; for out of it wast thou taken: for dust thou art, and unto dust shalt thou return" (Genesis 3:17-19).

7. If Adam and Eve had not sinned, they and all mankind would never have had to experience disease nor death. Death came on mankind through Sin. Disease, which is incipient death, also

entered into the world by sin.

"As by one man sin entered into the world, and death by sin; and so death passed upon all men, for that all have sinned..." (Romans 5:12).

But never fear, God is here!

"God was in Christ, reconciling the world unto himself, not imputing their trespasses unto them..." (II Corinthians 5:19).

"For the wages of sin is death; but the gift of God is eternal life through Jesus Christ our Lord" (Romans 6:23).

"Who his own self bare our sins in his own body on the tree, that we, being dead to sins, should live unto righteousness: by whose stripes (beatings) you were healed" (I Peter 2:24).

God Created Man with Natural Healing Built into His Physical Body

8. Man's natural body has the capability to heal itself eight out of ten times! This is natural healing, built into our physical bodies by our Creator.

King David wrote, "I will praise thee; for I am fearfully and wonderfully made; marvelous are thy works; and that my soul knows right well" (Psalm 139:14). If we eat the right foods, exercise, rest, and stay free from stress, nature itself will work to heal our body. Yes, even after sin entered the world and defiled mankind, eight out of ten times our bodies can heal themselves.

9. Medical doctors assist nature through natural and artificial treatments, but cannot heal apart from the body's natural ability, and God's mercy.

Doctors have been given the ability from God to find, understand, and use natural substances from the earth and create medicines which help the body fight disease, and in many cases, experience natural healing. They can also take more desperate measures by operating and removing body parts and diseased or infected tumors and growths. In many cases, healing is encouraged and achieved very slowly, and with great suffering and expense, and in some very difficult situations, doctors experiment to find the cause or simply treat symptoms and hope for results. But when nature fails, and man's best efforts with modern medicine fail, what power is strong enough to heal the body? Naturally speaking, if sickness is allowed to advance beyond the ability of the individual to practice good natural diet, exercise, and rest, or the ability of doctors to implement modern medical means, the result will always be death, unless the disease is removed supernaturally by faith.

"O wretched man that I am! Who shall deliver me from the body of this death? I thank God through Jesus Christ our Lord" (Romans 7:24-25).

JESUS IS THE HEALER

Healing was Purchased by Christ's Atonement

10. God's provision for Divine Healing takes into account the fact that disease entered the world through the curse of Sin, and one must deal with the Sin to get rid of the disease.

If the curse of sin, sickness and death came as judgment, who can remove that curse and that judgment but God? The question is, Can God remove it *now*? *In this life*? Yes!

In fact, *<u>God has already removed the curse of sin</u> and sickness, through the perfect sacrifice of His Son, Jesus Christ!*

"For God so loved the world, He <u>gave</u> His only begotten Son, that whosoever believeth in him should not perish, but have everlasting life" (John 3:16).

"Christ <u>has redeemed</u> us from the curse of the law, being made a curse for us: for it is written, Cursed is every one that hangs on a tree (cross of crucifixion): That the blessing of Abraham might come on the Gentiles through Jesus Christ; that we might receive the promise of the Spirit through faith" (Galatians 3:13-14).

"Wherefore, as by one man (Adam) sin entered into the world, and death by sin; and so death passed upon all men, for that all have sinned…but not as the offense, so also is the free gift. For if through the offence of one many be dead, much more the grace of God, and the gift by grace, which is by one man, Jesus Christ, <u>hath abounded</u> unto many" (Romans 5:12,17).

"For the law of the Spirit of life in Christ Jesus <u>has made me free</u> from the law of sin and death" (Romans 8:2).

"Who <u>his own self bare our sins</u> in his own body on the tree (cross), that we, being dead to sins, should live unto righteousness: by whose stripes <u>ye were healed</u>" (I Peter 2:24).

Notice that the underlined verbs in these passages are past tense. God speaks in past tense because the price has already been paid, life for life, the blood of righteous Jesus for the sins and sicknesses of "whosoever will" among men!

Why do we still see sin, sickness and death? Sickness and death would vanish in all the world if sinning could be eliminated. In fact, when the end of the ages has come, and this world passes away, God will establish His eternal kingdom, and there will be no more disease or pain or death. "And God shall wipe away all tears from their eyes; and there shall be no more death, neither sorrow, nor crying, neither shall there be any more pain: for the former things are passed away" (Revelation 21:4).

But right now, by faith, we can pray, "Thy kingdom come, thy will be done in earth as it is in heaven" (Matthew 6:10). How is God's will in heaven? That's right, it is perfect! No sin, no sickness, no sadness, no separation. So we can pray and believe to see his will done in earth as it is already done in heaven – perfect!

God's "Roman" Road

The Apostle Paul wrote two-thirds of the New Testament, and the book of Romans is his masterpiece of explaining God' amazing plan of salvation. Let's walk through Romans and travel what scholars call "The Roman Road" of Salvation.

1. All men are guilty before God.

   - **Romans 3:10** "There is none righteous, no, not one."

2. All men have committed sin.

   - **Romans 3:23** "For all have sinned, and come short of the glory of God."

3. God outdid Himself by loving us when we were sinners.

JESUS IS THE HEALER

- **Romans 5:8** "God commendeth his love toward us, in that, while were yet sinners, Christ died for us."

4. Death for all men comes because of sin, but God's free gift is eternal life through Jesus Christ.

   - **Romans 6:23** "For the wages of sin is death; but the gift of God is eternal life through Jesus Christ our Lord."

5. We accept God's gift of life by believing in our heart and speaking with our mouth that Jesus Christ paid the price of God's justice.
6.
   - **Romans 10:9-10** "That if you shall confess with your mouth the Lord Jesus, and shall believe in your heart that God has raised him from the dead, you shall be saved. For with the heart man believeth unto righteousness; and with the mouth confession is made unto salvation."

7. God saves those who sincerely call upon him.

   - **Romans 10:13** "For whosoever shall call upon the name of the Lord shall be saved."

Chapter One
Review Questions

Why is Sickness in the World?

1. The entrance of _____ through _____ opened the door to disease. The same event that allowed sin to enter the world also allowed sickness and disease to enter.

    Genesis 1:26

    Genesis 2:17

    Genesis 3:1-19

2. God's Roman Road to Salvation:

    1)

    2)

    3)

    4)

    5)

    6)

JESUS IS THE HEALER

3. If everyone living was a doctor, if every home on earth was a hospital, why would there still be sickness, disease and death in the world?

___

4. Why is Satan the author of sickness and disease?

___

TERRY KINARD

2

DEALING WITH SIN AND SICKNESS

How do we deal with sin and sickness, and all the evils that come with the curse?

1. We must deal with sin in our lives first, before we seek God for healing.

Remember, you can go to Heaven with sickness in your body, but you cannot go to Heaven with sin in your heart.

All of mankind is under the curse of sin. No one can be good enough to enter Heaven. Our only hope is in the sacrifice of the perfect Son of God, the Lord Jesus Christ. "There is none righteous, no, not one: There is none that understandeth, there is none that seeketh after God. They are all gone out of the way, they are together become unprofitable; there is none that doeth good, no, not one" (Romans 3:9). "For all have sinned, and come short of the glory of God" (Romans 3:23). "All we like sheep have gone astray; we have turned every one to his own way; and the Lord hath laid on him (Jesus) the iniquity (tendency to sin) of us all" (Isaiah 53:6).

2. Because we are all born under the curse, we are doomed to spend eternity in torment, separated from a holy God.

"For the wages of sin is death; but the gift of God is eternal life through Jesus Christ our Lord" (Romans 6:23). "O wretched man that I am! Who shall deliver me from the body of this death? I thank God through Jesus Christ our Lord" (Romans 7: 24-25).

We Must Repent

3. God has done His part to save us, and more.

In fact, "God commendeth (exhibited the completeness of) His love toward us, in that, while we were yet sinners, Christ died for us. Much more then, being now justified by his blood, we shall be saved from wrath through him" (Romans 5:8-9). "For God so loved the world, He gave His only begotten Son, that whosoever believeth in Him, should not perish, but have everlasting life" (John 3:16).

4. We must do our part to be saved. We must come to God, repent of (turn away from) our sin, and ask His forgiveness.

God calls, and continually makes the offer of freedom, but we must choose to come to Him if we would receive the gift of life, which only He can give. "For the grace of God which bringeth salvation hath appeared to all men, teaching us that, denying ungodliness and worldly lusts, we should live soberly, righteously, and godly, in this present world..." (Titus 2:11-12). "Repent ye therefore, and be converted (changed, transformed), that your sins may be blotted out, when the times of refreshing shall come from the presence of the Lord"

(Acts 3:19). "And it shall come to pass, that whosoever shall call on the name of the Lord shall be saved" (Acts 2:21).

Where Will You Spend Eternity?

5. Death is not the end. Man is an eternal being. And forever is a very long time.

Even though death passed upon man as far as the earth is concerned, the spirit of man will live eternally, either in the presence of God and the holy angels, or in the presence of the devil and his demons. Jesus said, "Except ye repent, ye shall all likewise perish" (Luke 13:5).

Can we wait until we get to Heaven to be saved? No, we only have this life to make a decision to live for God, to make our decision to invite Him into our heart, and to ask Him to forgive us and be our Lord and Master. Once we cross over the line of death into eternity, it is too late. "and if the tree fall toward the south, or toward the north, in the place where the tree falleth, there it shall be" (Ecclesiastes 11:3). In other words, as the tree falls, so shall it lie. Whatever state you are in when you die, that is sealed and set for all eternity. That is why inspired gospel writers pleaded,

"Today, if ye will hear His voice, harden not your heart" (Hebrews 3:7-8).

Adam and Eve disobeyed God and brought the curse of sin on all mankind. Yet God, in His tender love and mercy, sent His only Son into the earth, to live a sinless life, so He could be the perfect sacrifice to satisfy the justice of a holy God. We can never satisfy God's justice apart from the sacrifice of Jesus Christ, the Son of God. The price has been paid; the way has been made. All that remains is for us to humble ourselves, repent, and ask God's forgiveness. Simply pray this simple prayer sincerely from your heart:

Prayer of Repentance for Salvation

Dear Heavenly Father,
I come to you in the name of your Son, Jesus Christ, and ask you to forgive me of all my sin. I repent, I turn away from sins, and I give my life to you. From this day forward I will live for you, and you will be my God. Come into my heart, Lord Jesus, and take control. I receive you as my Lord and
Master, my deliverer, my provider, and my healer. Thank you, Lord Jesus, for saving my soul. Thank you for forgiving me. I worship you, Lord, and I love you. Amen.

Review Questions
Chapter 2

DEALING WITH SIN AND SICKNESS

1. What is God's judgment for sin?

   _____
   _____
   _____
   _____
   _____

2. How did God completely show His love for mankind?

   _____
   _____
   _____
   _____
   _____

3. What must we do to be saved?

   _____
   _____
   _____
   _____
   _____

4. Can we wait until we die to ask God to forgive us and save us?

_____
_____
_____
_____
_____

3

BIBLICAL BASIS FOR DIVINE HEALING

God is not the Author of Sickness.

As we have shown previously, sickness is part of the curse that came into the world as a direct result of sin. Sickness is the work of the devil. If you believe sickness is from God, you are not very likely to look to Him for your healing. But if you realize that sickness is from the devil, then you can look to God. "For this purpose the Son of God was manifested, that he might destroy <u>the works of the devil</u>" (I John 3:8). We also see in the word, "How God anointed Jesus of Nazareth with the Holy Ghost and with power, who went about doing good, and healing all who were <u>oppressed of the devil</u>, for God was with him" (Acts 10:38). We see then, that sickness is the work of the devil, and that he uses sickness to oppress mankind.

The prophet Isaiah asked, "Who hath believed our report? And to whom is the arm of the Lord revealed?" (Isaiah 53:1) "Surely He (Jesus) hath borne our griefs (sicknesses in the original Hebrew), and carried our sorrows (pains): yet we did esteem him stricken, smitten of God, and afflicted. But He was wounded for our transgressions, He was bruised for our iniquities: the chastisement of our peace was upon Him; and with <u>his stripes we are healed</u>" (Isaiah 53:4) Isaiah looked forward to the Cross by faith. Later, Peter declared, "Who his own self bare our sins in his own body on the tree, <u>by whose stripes ye were healed</u>" (I Peter 2:24). Peter was looking back to the Cross by faith.

The promises are to those who believe the report of God about His Son, Jesus. If you believe Jesus is the Savior, you will be saved. If you believe He is the Healer, you will be healed. If you believe He is the Baptizer in the Holy Ghost, you can receive the power of the infilling of the Holy Ghost. If you believe he is the Deliverer from bondage, you will be delivered. If you believe He is your Provider, your needs will be met. "For in Him we live, and move, and have our being" (Acts 17:28). "In Him was life; and the life was the light of men" (John 1:4).

Jesus returned to His home town of Nazareth, entered the synagogue, and was handed the book (the Old Testament scriptures) to read. Jesus turned to the book of Isaiah and read "the Spirit of the Lord is upon me, for He hath anointed me <u>to preach the gospel</u> to the poor; he hath sent me <u>to heal</u> the broken hearted, <u>to preach deliverance</u> to the captives, and <u>recovering of sight</u> to the blind, <u>to set at liberty</u> them that are bruised; <u>to preach the acceptable year of the Lord</u>" (Luke 4:16-22, quoting Isaiah 61:1-2). He gave the book back saying, "This day is this scripture fulfilled in your ears…And all bare Him witness, and wondered at the <u>gracious words</u> that proceeded out of his mouth" (Luke 4:22).

Gracious words are words of blessing. And Jesus came to bring blessing. It's interesting that there are six things mentioned in the passage that Jesus came to do, and six is the biblical number for man. Jesus came to bless mankind. It all can be summed up in I John 3:8, which says "For this purpose was the Son of God manifested, that he might destroy the works of the devil." And although they heard Jesus' words, they did not respond in faith, and Jesus marveled at their unbelief (Matthew 13:58).

Mark records of the same occasion, that Jesus responded, "A prophet is not without honor, but in his own country, and among his own kin, and in his own house. And He could there do no mighty work, save that He laid his hands upon a few sick folk, and healed them. And He marveled because of their unbelief. And He went round about the villages, teaching" (Mark 6:4-6; Matthew 13:57-58).

The Atmosphere Affects Healing

The atmosphere around the word and prayer can be conducive to God moving, or not conducive to God moving. If we enter an atmosphere of worship, and sit down, and do not reach out in faith, nothing may happen because of our attitude, and we may also hinder someone else from receiving too. Our level of faith is very important in receiving healing from God. "If you can believe, all things are possible to him that believeth" (Mark 9:23).

One day Jesus was teaching a diverse group of people concerning the Kingdom of God, and the Word says, "and the power of the Lord was present to heal them" (Luke 5:17). The atmosphere can be one of faith, inviting the Lord to work mightily. On another occasion, the apostle Paul was preaching the gospel at Lystra, and a man who was impotent in his feet (crippled) "being a cripple from his mother's womb, who never had walked: The same heard Paul speak: who steadfastly beholding him, and perceiving that he had faith to be healed, said with a loud voice, Stand upright on thy feet. And he leaped and walked" (Acts 14:8-9). In this instance, only one man was healed, but he had heard the gospel*, and received faith for his miracle.

*Paul must have been preaching God's power to heal as well as forgive, since the crippled man received faith for healing by hearing the gospel. The full gospel includes divine healing. "And they went forth, and preached everywhere, the Lord working with them, and confirming the word with signs following" (Mark 16:20).

The atmosphere of faith is directly affected by the individual level of faith in the people present. In other words, if you have a room full of untaught, lukewarm, half-hearted Christians, don't expect to see the power of God manifested. Even Jesus could "do there no mighty work...and He marveled because of their unbelief" (Mark 6:5-6).

"We ought to give the more earnest heed to the things we have heard, lest we let them slip...How shall we escape, if we neglect so great salvation; which at the first began to be spoken by the Lord, and was confirmed unto us by them that heard him; God also bearing them witness, both with signs and wonders, and with divers miracles, and gifts of the Holy Ghost, according to his own will?" (Hebrews 2:1,3-4).

The answer is, we will not escape. Many precious Christians have died and gone to be with the Lord because they let valuable truths about God's promises "slip," and so were unable to inherit the promises. "Be not slothful (lazy, dull), but followers of them who through faith and patience inherit the promises" (Hebrews 6:12).

Truth Can Become Dormant in Us

Truths we've known can become dormant, dead doctrine, not alive in our spirit anymore. In Genesis 26, Abraham had dug wells in the desert, and after his death, the enemy had stopped them up. Isaac, Abraham's son, came and dug them out again. Those wells were places of refreshing that had ceased to flow, and needed to be redug. The Word records why those wells were not flowing "the Philistines (the enemy) had stopped them, and filled them with earth" (Genesis 26:15). When our lives become too filled up with the things of this earth, the flow of the Spirit of God, the "living water," is hindered, or even stopped.

"Therefore with joy shall we draw water from the wells of salvation" (Isaiah 12:3). We need to "dig out" the well of healing, and get the blessing flowing to God's people again. "And Isaac digged again the wells of water, which they had digged in the days of Abraham his father...and he called their names after the names by which his father had called them" (Genesis 26:18).

We're talking about digging out the spiritual wells of salvation, and allowing the living water of healing to flow to God's people. Notice that when Isaac redug the wells of his father, he called them by the same names that Abraham had called them.

Those names were Esek (Genesis 26:20) which means "strife"; Sitnah (v 21) which means "contention"; and Rehoboth (v 22) which means "room" and "fruitful." The lesson is that we all come into the atmosphere of true faith the same way, digging through "earth," the things of this earthly life which grab our time and attention, and are so easily used by the devil to stop the flow of God's promises in our life. In that process of breaking through into God's blessing, the enemy is not sitting idly by. We will encounter "strife," and "contention." There will always be opposition from this world, when we press into the supernatural flow of God's blessings. But keep on digging! Because the final resting place is "Rehoboth," which means God will make room for us in the land of our affliction, and He will make us fruitful in the land. We cannot lose, if we do not quit!

"There is a river; the streams thereof make glad the city of God" (Psalm 46:4). Streams are tributaries which flow from the main source, and Healing is one of those streams. It needs to flow, because it brings joy and gladness to the house of God. We who understand need to get it flowing again to God's people. "The people that do know their God shall be strong, and do exploits. And they that understand among the people shall instruct many" (Daniel 11:32:33).

There are doctrinal statements we as Christians profess to believe, like the Baptism in the Holy Ghost. But the majority of people are not filled with the Baptism in the Holy Ghost. We believe in Divine Healing, but it is not flowing to God's people. We say we believe in the Second Coming of the Lord Jesus, yet many people live like they don't! These streams need to be dug out again, so they can flow to God's people. Until then, they are merely doctrinal statements, not affecting our lives.

There is nothing wrong with our doctrinal statements, but if the truth of those statements is not flowing, it does not profit God's people. Any word must be believed to be effective in our lives; otherwise, we will not act upon it. "For unto us was the gospel preached, as well as unto them: but the word preached did not profit them, not being mixed with faith in them that heard it" (Hebrews 4:2). The gospel includes healing for our bodies. Jesus not only forgives sin, he also heals sickness. His death paid the price of our redemption, spirit, soul, and body. He died for us, and we should live for Him.

Healing Glorifies God

We should glorify God in our spirit and in our body, which are the Lord's. We glorify God in our spirit by living above the dominion of sin. And we glorify God in our body by living above the dominion of sickness, and living in health.

"For you are bought with a price: therefore glorify God in your body and in your spirit, which are God's" (I Corinthians 6:20). "Whether therefore ye eat, or drink, or whatsoever ye do, do all to the glory of God" (I Corinthians 10:31). "But he that glorieth, let him glory in the Lord" (I Corinthians 10:17).

Think of it this way. Your body is the possession of God. And if your body is the possession of God, He wants the devil loosed off your body. God wants you free from sickness. "Beloved , I wish above all things that thou mayest prosper and be in health, even as thy soul prospereth" (III John 1:2).

We are Redeemed From
The Curse of Sin and Sickness

"Christ hath redeemed us from the curse of the law, being made a curse for us: for it is written, Cursed is every one who hangeth on a tree: That the blessing of Abraham might come on the Gentiles through Jesus Christ; that we might receive the promise of the Spirit through faith" (Galatians 3:13-14).

When Jesus hung on the Cross, He bore the curse of the law on our behalf. He became cursed, so we can be blessed. "For he (the Father) hath made Him (Jesus) to be sin for us, who knew no sin; that we might be made the righteousness of God <u>in him</u>" (II Corinthians 5:21). "If any man be <u>in Christ</u>, he is a new creature; old things are passed away, behold, all things are become new" (II Corinthians 5:17).

Jesus redeemed us from the curse of the law, being made a curse for us, for it is written, 'Cursed is every one that hangeth on a tree.' What is the "curse of the law?" In Deuteronomy 28, we read about the curses (verses 15-67) and the blessings (verses 1-14) of the law. Curses included every sickness and disease that is written in the law, and every sickness and disease that is NOT written in the law.

Specifically, the Word says, "the Lord will make thy plagues wonderful (distinctly difficult and too hard), and the plagues of thy seed (children), even great plagues (a blow, wound, pestilence), and of long continuance, and sore sicknesses, and of long continuance. Moreover he will bring upon thee all the diseases of Egypt, which thou wast afraid of; and they shall cleave unto thee. Also every sickness, and every plague, which is not written in the book of this law, them will the Lord bring upon thee, until thou be destroyed...and thy life shall hang in doubt before thee; and thou shalt fear day and night, and shalt have none assurance of thy life: In the morning thou shalt say, Would God it were even! And at even thou shalt say, Would God it were morning! For the fear of thine heart wherewith thou shalt fear, and for the sight of thine eyes which thou shalt see..." (Deuteronomy 28:59-61; 66-67).

All sickness and disease is part of the curse of the law. Jesus became a curse for us. Jesus redeemed us from the curse of the law, which includes every sickness and disease, known, or unknown, to mankind. "Himself took our infirmities and bare our sicknesses"(Matthew 8:17). "Surely He hath borne our griefs (sicknesses), and carried our sorrows (pains)...He was wounded for our transgressions (sins), he was bruised for our iniquities (the inward nature or tendency to sin): the chastisement of our peace was upon him; and with his stripes we are healed" (Isaiah 53:4-5). "Who His own self bare our sins in his own body on the tree (the Cross), that we, being dead to sins, should live unto righteousness: <u>by whose stripes ye were healed</u>" (I Peter 2:24).

"But," you say, "If Christ has redeemed us fully, from both sin and sickness, why do we get sick? How can we receive a plague, (a blow, a wound, pestilence)? If we are truly redeemed, how can these things come upon us?

Why Do the Redeemed Get Sick?

We are redeemed by faith in the blood of Jesus, shed on Calvary for our forgiveness. With His blood, He paid the penalty of sin, and we are free. He also paid the price for our healing, and we can live in divine health. We came into His divine life by faith, and we stand in His life by faith (a right reaction to God's ability). But we have not yet received the final form of our redemption for our spirit, or our body.

We have not received the final redemption of our physical body. "We know that the whole creation groaneth and travaileth in pain together until now. And not only they, but ourselves also, which have the first fruits of the Spirit, even we ourselves groan within ourselves, <u>waiting for the adoption, to wit, the redemption of our body</u>. For we are saved by hope" (Romans 8:22-24). In the future, there is an "adoption, (that is, the) redemption of the body, at the resurrection" (Romans 8:23). "Behold, I show you a mystery; We shall not all sleep (die), but we shall all be changed...For this corruptible must put on incorruption, and this mortal must put on immortality...then shall be brought to pass the saying that is written, Death is swallowed up in victory. O death, where is thy sting? O grave, where is thy victory? The sting of death is sin, and the strength of sin is the law. But thanks be to God, which giveth us the victory through our Lord Jesus Christ. Therefore, my beloved brethren, be ye steadfast, unmovable, always abounding in the work of the Lord, forasmuch as ye know that your labor is not in vain in the Lord" (I Corinthians 15:51-58).

The fullness of our physical bodily redemption is in the future. We wait for the Second Coming of the Lord, to receive the fullness of redemption for the body. This mortal will put on immortality. This corruptible will put on incorruption. " And God will wipe away all tears from their eyes; and there shall be no more death, neither sorrow, nor crying, neither shall there be any more pain: for the former things are passed away" (Revelation 21:4). Because the fullness of redemption for our physical body lies in the future, we know we are never in a position in this life where we cannot be tempted to be sick; where it is not possible to be wounded, or plagued, or hurt.

But consider this:
We're also redeemed from sin, and the fullness of that also awaits future resurrection. Paul tells us, "receiving the end of your faith, even the salvation of your souls" (I Peter 1:9). We are never in a position in this life where we cannot be tempted to sin, or where it is not possible for us to sin. Our life is a daily walk of faith. But that fact does not relieve us from the responsibility or challenge to resist sin, and not let sin have dominion over us! "For sin shall not have dominion over you: for ye are not under the law, but under grace (God's underserved favor and ability made available to man)" (Romans 6:14).

Paul testified, "I am crucified with Christ, nevertheless I live; yet not I, but Christ liveth in me. And the life I now live in the flesh, I live by the faith of the Son of God, who loved me, and gave himself for me" (Galatians 2:20). Paul also said, "I die daily..." (I Corinthians 15:31). The fact that Jesus redeemed us with his blood from the power of sin does not relieve us from the responsibility to resist sin, and not let sin have dominion over us. What should we do? "Reckon ye also yourselves to be dead indeed unto sin, but alive unto God through Jesus Christ our Lord. Let not sin therefore reign in your mortal body, that ye should obey it in the lusts thereof. Neither yield ye your members (your body) as instruments of unrighteousness unto sin: but yield yourselves unto God, as those that are alive from the dead, and your members as instruments of righteousness unto God" (Romans 6:11-13).

"Be sober, be vigilant; because your adversary the devil, as a roaring lion, walketh about, seeking whom he MAY devour" (I Peter 5:8). The word "may" here is in the permissive sense, meaning that Satan has to have your permission to devour you! JUST SAY NO! Say "No!" to sin in your life, and say "No!" to sickness in your life! Take your authority in the name of Jesus Christ!

We see then, that <u>it is our responsibility to resist sin in our lives, because Jesus paid the price for our redemption from sin</u>. We are not yet finally delivered from sin, but we are delivered from its dominion, and we can resist and overcome it. Isn't it also logical to say the same about sickness? I asked Jesus to forgive me when I got saved. Yet, I've had to ask Him a few times to forgive me since I did get saved! I asked Jesus to heal me when I got saved. And I've had to ask Him to heal me since I did get saved! But as I learn to walk in the benefits of my redemption, the times when I have to ask forgiveness should become fewer and
farther between. In the same way, the times when I need to ask for healing should get fewer and farther between.

We are the possession of God, and He wants us free, body, soul, and spirit.

He wants sin loosed off our lives.
He wants sickness loosed off our lives.
He wants distress loosed off our lives.

But we must cooperate with Him and resist, through faith, through trusting in His atoning death and resurrection, that the power of God prevails for us. John said, "these things write I unto you, that ye sin not. And <u>if any man sin</u>, we have an advocate with the Father, Jesus Christ the righteous" (I John 2:1). "If we confess our sins, he is faithful and just to forgive us our sins, and to cleanse us from all unrighteousness" (I John 1:9).

It is not God's will for us to sin. But John says, IF ANY MAN SIN. If God expected us to sin, he would have said, WHEN ANY MAN SINS, but he said "IF". "IF" is the exception to the rule, not the normal course of events. We can live above sin, one day at a time. But IF we do sin, we have an advocate, an attorney, a mediator, with the Father, Christ Jesus the righteous. And when we confess our sins to Him with heartfelt godly sorrow, He forgives us and cleanses us, and justifies us (just as if we never sinned).

If sin for the believer is the exception and not the rule, why wouldn't it be the same for sickness?

I was Forgiven when I got saved!
I was Healed when I got saved!
I've been Forgiven since I got saved!
I've been Healed since I got saved!
Why don't we get as determined about sickness as we have been about sin, and declare: "Sin is not the will of God for the believer. Sickness is not the will of God for the believer.
Lord, you forgave me in the past.
Lord, you healed me in the past.
Lord, forgive me now.
Lord, heal me now."

"<u>Heal me</u>, O Lord, and I shall be healed; <u>save me</u>, and I shall be saved: for thou art my praise" (Jeremiah 17:14). "Bless the Lord, O my soul: and all that is within me, bless his holy name. (2) Bless the Lord, O my soul, and forget not all his benefits: (3)<u>Who forgiveth all thine iniquities; who healeth all thy diseases</u>. (4)Who redeemeth thy life from destruction; who crowneth thee with lovingkindness and tender mercies; (5) Who satisfieth thy mouth with good things; so that thy youth is renewed like the eagle's" (Psalm 103:1-5

Review Questions
Chapter 3

BIBLICAL BASIS FOR DIVINE HEALING

1. Who oppresses people with sickness, according to Acts 10:38?

2. To whom are these promises of healing made? (Isaiah 53:4 "with his stripes we are healed") and (I Peter 2:24 "by whose stripes ye were healed.")

4

HEALING IS A TEMPORAL BLESSING

The most important decision in life is knowing your sins are forgiven, and you are born again, and you are fitted to go to Heaven. But we must not limit what Jesus came to do just to the eternal realm, and just to the fact that we get to go to heaven if we're a true believer in Jesus Christ.

God is interested in our lives here on earth. Yes, He is most interested in the spiritual, but He is also interested in the temporal (or temporary). <u>Healing is a temporal blessing</u>. Healing is an earthly blessing. It's a blessing we experience this side of heaven. We won't need healing in heaven, because there is no sickness there.

That's another reason we can know God wants to heal people, because He told us to pray "thy kingdom come, thy will be done, in earth, as it is in heaven" (Matthew 6:10). Now we know the fullness of God's will in the earth will not be accomplished in this present age, but we can "taste" the powers of the world to come. Hebrews 6:5 "And have tasted the good word of God, and the powers of the world to come." There can be healing right now, this side of heaven.

Another reason we know God heals today is by the meaning of the word "saved." The Bible clearly tells us "whosoever shall call upon the name of the Lord shall be saved" (Romans 10:13). The word "saved" carries in its meaning more than just the forgiveness of sin. It indicates soundness, healing, deliverance, blessing, provision. Consider what Peter wrote "According as his divine power hath given unto us all things that pertain to life and godliness, through the knowledge of him that hath called us to glory and virtue" (II Peter 1:3).

Whatever we need that relates to this present life, and living victoriously for God, He has provided through His power, and we access these provisions through understanding who He is and how He loves mankind.

The New Testament is full of incidents of divine healing. When Jesus was here on earth, there was healing, and the Bible plainly declares that Jesus Christ is the "same yesterday, today, and forever" (Hebrews 13:8). The word declares "how God anointed Jesus of Nazareth with the Holy Ghost and with power: who went about doing good, and healing all that were oppressed of the devil; for God was with Him" (Acts 10:38). If Jesus was the Healer when He was on earth, He is still the Healer today. Remember, He said, "I am the Lord, I change not" (Malachi 3:6).

People Must Hear the Gospel

Someone has to tell people that Jesus loves them, died for them, and has power to bless, deliver, save, and heal. Why does God send preachers into the earth? God sends His servants to the people of the world to tell them the Gospel, or good news, that He loves mankind, and has provided the way to redeem us from the curse, to forgive us of sin, and to give us eternal life.

But that is not all! All the blessings in this life come from the goodness of God. "Every good gift and every perfect gift is from above, and cometh down from the Father of lights, with whom is no variableness, neither shadow of turning" (James 1:17). You say, "Does God bless the unrighteous, non-believer, as well as the Christian?" Yes, He does. The Bible says "he maketh his sun to rise on the evil and on the good, and sendeth rain on the just and on the unjust" (Matthew 5:45). In His field, He lets the tares (weeds) and wheat grow together until the harvest.

Jesus explained the parable, or story, in Matthew 13:40-43, "He (Jesus) answered...As therefore the tares are gathered and burned in the fire; so shall it be in the end of this world. The Son of man shall send forth his angels, and they shall gather out of his kingdom all things that offend, and them which do iniquity; and shall cast them into a furnace of fire: there shall be wailing and gnashing of teeth. Then shall the righteous shine forth as the sun in the kingdom of their Father. Who hath ears to hear, let him hear."
All men enjoy God's good creation and good gifts in this life to some extent. But in the end, He will separate the believers from the unbelievers, and punish those who did not receive Him according to His righteous judgments. Where we stand on that day is up to us. God is loving and patient, giving men time to hear and repent. He calls to you and to me, "Come now, and let us reason together,

saith the Lord: though your sins be as scarlet, they shall be as white as snow; though they be red like crimson, they shall be as wool. If ye be willing and obedient, ye shall eat the good of the land: But if ye refuse and rebel, ye shall be devoured with the sword: for the mouth of the Lord hath spoken it" (Isaiah 1:18-20).

He tells us in Romans 10:13-15 "For whosoever shall call upon the name of the Lord shall be saved. How then shall they call on him in whom they have not believed? And how shall they believe in him (Jesus) of whom they have not heard? And how shall they hear without a preacher? And how shall they preach, except they be sent? As it is written, How beautiful are the feet of
 them that preach the gospel of peace, and bring glad tidings of good things!

Notice that "tidings" and "things" are plural. Salvation includes more than just forgiveness of sin. There are many glad tidings that come with the gospel (good news) of Jesus Christ, and healing is one of those blessings. Your journey toward healing begins with faith in God for salvation.

JESUS IS THE HEALER

Review Questions
Chapter 4

HEALING IS A TEMPORAL BLESSING

1. What kind of blessing is health and healing?

___

2. Why is healing a temporal blessing?

___

3. What is the "Full Gospel" message from God to mankind?

___

4. What has to happen for God's will to be done in earth as it is in Heaven?

5. What does the word "saved" actually mean?

6. Why does God send preachers into the earth?

7. Why are evil men blessed?

_____
_____
_____
_____
_____
_____

TERRY KINARD

5

HEALING IS A COVENANT PROMISE

The first covenant promise that God made with His people, after delivering them from Egypt, was a covenant of healing. What happened to God's people in the Old Testament is a picture, a type, a shadow, of the redemption of the Lord Jesus for us today, under the New Testament. Speaking of the two parts of our Bible, we could say:

> The New is in the Old contained,
> The Old is by the New explained;
> The New is in the Old concealed,
> The Old is by the New revealed;
> The New is in the Old enfolded,
> The Old is by the New unfolded.

The Old and New Testaments make up one book, the Holy Bible, which speaks in totality of the love of God, and the full redemption He declared through the life, death, and resurrection of His Son, Jesus Christ. "Now all these things happened to them (God's people in the Old Testament) for ensamples (a live model, a type, for imitation):and they are written for our admonition, upon whom the ends of the world are come" (I Corinthians 10:11). So God's covenant promises to Old Testament Israel are valid examples for us to receive and follow today. Consider this first covenant promise He made, which promised healing.

The people of God had journeyed to a place called "Marah," where the waters were bitter. Moses cried to the Lord, and the Lord showed him a tree (picture of the Cross and Redemption), which, when he had cast into the waters, the waters were made sweet: (When we receive Jesus and His redemption at the Cross, our lives become sweet, and the bitterness of sin is broken.) ….there He (God) made for them a statute and an ordinance, and there He proved them, and said, If thou wilt diligently hearken to the voice of the Lord thy God, and wilt do that which is right in his sight, and wilt give ear (listen to) His commandments, and keep (obey) all his statutes, I will put none of these diseases upon thee, which I have brought upon the Egyptians (type of unbelievers): for I am the Lord that healeth thee" (Exodus 15:25-26).

This covenant reveals one of God's many "I AM" names. The name is Jehovah Rapha, which means, The LORD your physician (doctor). Who is your family doctor?

These scriptures in Exodus show us that God wanted His people delivered from Egypt (a type of the world system of unbelievers), and He also wanted them healed.

The Passover Covenant

In Exodus chapter twelve, we read about the Passover, the night in which the final plague against Pharaoh of Egypt brought the release of God's people from over 400 years of slavery and bondage. God told his people to put the blood of a spotless lamb (which pictures the sacrifice of Jesus, the Lamb of God) over the doorposts of their homes (Exodus 12:7), and when the death angel passed through the land, He would "pass over" the ones who had applied the blood of the lamb. (Exodus 12:13) What a glorious "ensample" or "type" of our salvation! But not only did God tell them to apply the blood to their homes, He also told them to EAT the Passover lamb, to take in into their physical bodies. "And they shall eat the flesh in that night…" (Exodus 12:8). And what was the result? "He brought them forth also with silver and gold: and there was not one feeble person among their tribes" (Psalm 105:37).

God provided forgiveness of sin.
God provided provision (material possessions).
God provided healing.
God has redeemed us body (healing), soul (provision), and spirit (forgiveness).

That was Old Testament covenant! The Word of God tells us that our New Testament covenant, secured with the blood of the Lord Jesus, is "a better covenant, which was established upon better promises" (Hebrews 8:6). If you can get healed under the Old Covenant, but you cannot get healed under the New Covenant, then the Old must be better! But God's Word says the New Covenant is better, established upon better promises!
Jesus is the Lamb of God that taketh away the sin of the world. (John 1:29) We trust His redeeming sacrifice of blood for forgiveness of our sin, (I Peter 1:18-19) and we trust His eternal life in us to heal us from sickness (I Peter 2:24). We must 'eat' or partake of the life of Jesus; that is, choose Him as the source of our strength and our life every day.

"Jesus said, I am the bread of life...I am the living bread which came down from heaven: If any man eat of this bread, he shall live for ever; and the bread that I will give is my flesh, which I will give for the life of the world...Jesus said, Except ye eat the flesh of the Son of God, and drink His blood, ye have no life in you...Many therefore of His disciples, when they had heard this, said, This is an hard saying; who can hear it? Jesus answered...the words that I speak unto you, they are spirit, and they are life" (John 6:48, 51-53,60,63). Do you hear Jesus' words? Do you see that salvation and redemption and deliverance, pictured by the Passover and Exodus from Egypt, point us to the finished work of the sinless Son of God?

Will you "eat His flesh", that is, <u>receive Him</u> into your life and heart as your sacrifice, as your "Passover" lamb, and will you reap the benefits of freedom from sin, from sickness, and from poverty? Moses told God's people, "I set before you this day, life and death, blessing and cursing. Choose life!" (Deuteronomy 30:19) Joshua declared, "Choose you this day whom you will serve. As for me and my house, we will serve the Lord" (Joshua 24:15).

The promises of healing and forgiveness are included together under God's covenant promises all through scripture. Jeremiah said, "<u>Heal me</u>, O Lord, and I shall be healed; <u>save me</u>, and I shall be saved: for thou art my praise" (Jeremiah 17:14). David wrote, "Bless the Lord, O my soul, and forget not all his benefits: Who <u>forgiveth all thine iniquities</u>; who <u>healeth all thy diseases</u>" (Psalm 103:2-3

6

Jesus and the Man with Palsy

Matthew 9:1-8

(1) And he entered into a ship, and passed over, and came into his own city.

(2) And, behold, they brought to him a man sick of the palsy, lying on a bed: and <u>Jesus seeing their faith said unto the sick of the palsy; son, be of good cheer; thy sins be forgiven thee.</u>

(3) And, behold, certain of the scribes said within themselves, This man blasphemeth.

(4) And Jesus knowing their thoughts said, Wherefore think ye evil in your hearts?

(5) <u>For whether is easier, to say, Thy sins be forgiven thee; or to say, Arise, and walk?</u>

(6) But that ye may know that the Son of man hath power on earth to forgive sins, (then saith he to the sick of the palsy,) Arise, take up thy bed, and go unto thine house.

(7) And he arose, and departed to his house.

(8) But when the multitudes saw it, (the healing), they marvelled, and glorified God, which had given such power unto men.

What did the Lord do for this sick man? Jesus not only <u>forgave</u> the man of his sins, He <u>healed</u> the man of palsy, and indicated that one was as easy to do as the other.

Now, most of us have no problem believing in God's forgiveness of our sins. Consider this scripture: "Therefore, if any man be in Christ, he is a new creature: old things are passed away; behold, all things are become new… <u>for he hath made him to be sin for us, who knew no sin; that we might be made the righteousness of God in him.</u>" (II Co 5:17,21).

God sent Jesus into the world to pay the ultimate sacrifice for us, to reconcile us to God, to pay the penalty for sin, so we could receive forgiveness and be saved. We are brought back into fellowship with God. We inherit eternal life through him, and we enjoy the benefits of son-ship while here on earth.

Jesus died for us, took our sin, to bring forgiveness, eternal life, and inheritance to us forever. We don't have a problem with that, do we?

Now consider: "Who his own self bare our sins in his own body on the tree, that we, being dead to sins, should live unto righteousness: by whose stripes <u>ye were healed</u>"

(I Peter 2:24) <u>Peter looked back</u> to the atoning death and resurrection of Jesus.

Consider Isaiah's opposite perspective on the other side of the Cross in the Old Testament. "With his stripes <u>we are healed</u>" (Isaiah 53:5) <u>Isaiah looked forward</u> by faith to the death and resurrection of Jesus, which would atone for our sins in the future. Both witnesses, Peter and Isaiah, confirm that Jesus paid the price for both forgiveness and healing.

Review Questions
Chapter 6

MAN HEALED OF PALSY

1. What two provisions of God are illustrated by the healing of the man with palsy in Matthew 9:1-8?

___
___
___
___
___
___

2. Which two writers speak of healing through the "stripes" (the beaten bloodied back) of the Lord Jesus?

___

3. What was each writer's perspective of the benefits of Jesus' atoning death on the Cross?

7

Mount Ebal and Mount Gerizim

When God's people entered the promised land, they passed between two mountains, with the road going in between. The mountains were Mount Ebal, the mount of cursing, and Mount Gerizim, the mount of blessing.

By commandment of the Lord, Moses appointed certain men to stand upon each of these mountains. As the people entered the Promised land, and passed by these mountains, the men were to proclaim God's blessings to the people from Mount Gerizim. These were the blessings they would receive if they obeyed His commandments. From Mount Ebal, other men proclaimed God's curses on the people if they disobeyed His commandments.

"Behold, <u>I set before you this day a blessing and a curse;</u> A blessing, if ye obey the commandments of the Lord your God, which I command you this day: And a curse, if ye will not obey the commandments of the Lord your God, but turn aside out of the way which I command you this day, to go after other gods, which ye have not known. And it shall come to pass, when the Lord thy God hath brought thee in unto the land whither thou goest to possess it, that thou <u>shalt put the blessing upon Mount Gerizim, and the curse upon Mount Ebal</u>" (Deuteronomy 11:26-29)

Remember, "now all these things happened unto them for ensamples (models, types): and they are written for our admonition (instruction), upon whom the ends of the world are come" (I Corinthians 10:11).

God had Moses place six representatives on each mountain, to proclaim His Word of blessing and cursing very plainly to the people, and they were without excuse. And so it is with us today. "These shall stand upon Mount Gerizim to bless the people... And these shall stand upon Mount Ebal to curse" (Deuteronomy 27:12,13). You can read the list of curses and blessings in Deuteronomy 27:15—28:67.

One of those blessings that was pronounced on the people was health and healing, as we read earlier, "If thou wilt diligently hearken to the voice of the Lord thy God, and wilt do that which is right in his sight, and wilt give ear to his commandments, and keep all his statutes, I will put none of these diseases upon thee, which I have brought upon the Egyptians: for I am the Lord that healeth thee" (Exodus 15:26).

We'll come back to these mountains of blessings and curses in a moment, but lets compare this account with a story in the New Testament.

Review Questions
Chapter 7

1. What were the meanings of the names of Mount Ebal and Mount Gerizim?

2. Why did Moses place representatives on each mountain to shout down curses and blessings on God's people?

TERRY KINARD

8

THE WOMAN AT THE WELL

One day, Jesus met a woman at the well of Jacob. "He left Judea, and departed again into Galilee. And he must needs (led of God to) go through Samaria...Now Jacob's well was there. Jesus therefore, being wearied with his journey, sat thus on the well...there cometh a woman of Samaria to draw water: Jesus saith unto her, Give me to drink...then saith the woman of Samaria unto him, How is it that thou, being a Jew, askest drink of me, which am a woman of Samaria? For the Jews have no dealing with the Samaritans" (John 4:3-9).

The Bible tells us He sat on the well, being weary with his journey. (John 4: 3-6) He was on His way back to Judea, and had stopped in this particular place, which was strange to other Jewish people. You see, this woman was a Samaritan, and the Samaritans were despised by the Jews.

The Samaritans were a mongrel (mixed breed) race of people that came about when the King of Assyria (who had conquered northern Israel), sent people from other countries to settle there in Samaria, which was the capital of Israel.

"And so it was at the beginning of their dwelling there, that they feared not the Lord: therefore the Lord sent lions among them, which slew some of them. Wherefore they spoke to the King of Assyria, saying, The nations which you have removed, and placed in the cities of Samaria, know not the manner of the God of the land: therefore he hath sent lions among them, and behold, they slay them, because they know not the manner of the God of the land. (They had a little sense, didn't they? They knew trouble comes when you do not honor God.) (II Kings 17:25-26)

Without going into great detail here, the King sent a priest down there, and he taught them the ways of God. (vv 27-28) However the Bible tells us they 'hedged' around true repentance. "Howbeit

(nevertheless) every nation made gods of their own, and put them in the houses of the high places which the Samaritans had made, every nation in their cities wherein they dwelt...so they feared the Lord (had respect of), and served their own gods,
after the manner of the nations whom they carried away from thence.

Unto this day they do (act) after the former manners. They fear not the Lord, neither do they (live) after their statutes, or after their ordinances, or after the law and commandment which the Lord commanded the children of Jacob, whom he named Israel...(II Kings 17: 29-34).

The Samaritans were like many people today, going through a form of godliness, showing a measure of respect to God, but continuing to serve other gods. The Samaritans even built their temple on Mount Gerizim, the Mount of Blessing (part of their form of worship...) They wanted God's blessing, but would not commit 100 percent to Him.

So the Samaritan woman at the well, in John chapter four, thinking she sounded religious, said to Jesus, "Sir, I perceive (my natural intuition tells me) that thou art a prophet. Our fathers worshipped in this mountain (Mount Gerizim); and ye say, that in Jerusalem is the place where men ought to worship" (John 4:19-20).

"Jesus saith unto her, Woman, believe me, the hour cometh, when ye shall neither in this mountain, nor yet at Jerusalem, worship the Father....But the hour cometh, and now is, when the <u>true worshippers</u> shall worship the Father in spirit and in truth; for the Father seeketh such to worship him" (John 4:21-23).

Jesus was giving instructions to the Samaritan woman about God's ways. True worshippers receive the blessing symbolized on Mount Gerizim, the Mount of Blessing. But the curses of Mount Ebal, the Mount of Cursing, still cling to all those who choose to rebel against the commandments of God.

The Bible tells us, "Be not deceived; God is not mocked: for whatsoever a man soweth, that shall he also reap" (Galatians 6:7). "This know also, that in the last days perilous times shall come...Having a form of godliness, but denying the power thereof: from such turn away" (II Timothy 3:1,5).

We cannot simply show respect, or follow a form of godliness, like the Samaritans, and expect God's blessing. We do not want God's curse, we want the blessing! Healing is a blessing! Forgiveness is a blessing!

Let's go back to the two mountains, Mount Ebal, the Mount of Cursing, and Mount Gerizim, the Mount of Blessing. They were designated by God to emphasize His will in the Old Testament. Then, in the New Testament, here comes Jesus. And He went to a place called Mount Calvary. And at Mount Calvary, Jesus merged Mount Ebal and Mount Gerizim! Jesus brought the curses and blessings together in His perfect sacrifice, and dealt with them at his crucifixion on Mount Calvary.

Mount Calvary became a mountain of cursing and a mountain of blessing. Jesus took the curses of Mount Ebal upon himself at Mount Calvary, so the blessing of Mount Gerizim could flow to you and to me through Mount Calvary!

Isn't that wonderful!?
"Christ hath redeemed us from the curse of the law, being made a curse for us...that the "blessing of Abraham might come on the Gentiles (that's us!) through Jesus Christ; that we might receive the promise of the Spirit through faith" (Galatians 3:13-14).

"And the Spirit and the bride (the Church) say, Come. And let him that heareth say, Come And let him that is athirst come. And whosoever will, let him take the water of life freely" (Revelation 22:17).

Review Questions
Chapter 8

THE WOMAN AT THE WELL

1. What group of people today does the woman at the well picture?

2. What was the significance of Jesus' visit with this woman?

3. Who were the Samaritans?

4. What happened to Mount Ebal and Mount Gerizim at Mt. Calvary?

_____
_____
_____
_____

9

HAS JESUS CHANGED?

If Jesus was the answer for life's problems when He walked on the earth, has He changed? He came from Heaven to Earth, and while He was here, He healed the sick, He forgave sins, He cast out devils, He comforted the discouraged, He strengthened the feeble minded, He sent out disciples to change the world. Has Jesus changed? Are the days of miracles and healings over?

Some have taught that miracles ceased when the last of Jesus' original twelve disciples (called apostles) died.

Pastor John Osteen told a story years ago which clearly proves this is not the case. He said, "Could you imagine what a scene that must have been, if miracles and healings were to pass away when the last apostle, John the Beloved, died? Can you see the desperation of people as John lay dying, saying, "Hurry, bring one more, so he can pray before he dies, because when he's gone, there will be no more miracles!" Think about it! Wouldn't that have been ridiculous, to think that the miracle working power of the God of the universe would end when the apostle John died?

Even if it were true that miracles would pass away when the last apostle died, the truth is, the last apostle is not dead! He's alive!

Because the first apostle is still alive! He, Jesus Christ, is the first and the last! He is "the apostle and high priest of our profession" (Hebrews 3:1), and He said, "Fear not; I am the first and the last: I am He that liveth, and was dead; and behold, I am alive forevermore!" (Revelation 1:18).

The Word of God also tells us that Jesus Christ is "the same yesterday, today, and forever" (Hebrews 13:8). And God the Father testified, saying, "I am the Lord, I change not…" (Malachi 3:6).

Jesus has not changed. He healed people when He was on earth, and He healed people after He ascended back to the Father. When Jesus Christ gave His disciples the Great Commission, He told them to continue the work He had begun, preaching and teaching the gospel of the Kingdom, including healing. He said, "Go ye into all the world, and preach the gospel to every creature. He that believeth and is baptized will be saved...these signs will follow them that believe: in My name they will cast out devils; they shall speak with new tongues; they shall take up serpents; and if they drink anything deadly, it shall not hurt them; they shall lay hands on the sick, and they shall recover (Mark 16:15-18).

Those who believe Jesus' word will cast out devils and pray and see healing for the sick. Some believe this commission was only for first century believers, but Jesus made it clear that His command was until the end of the age. "All power is given unto Me in heaven and in earth. Go ye therefore, and teach all nations...to observe all things whatsoever I have commanded you:

JESUS IS THE HEALER

and, lo, I am with you alway, even unto the end of the world" (Matthew 28:18-20).

The early church obeyed Jesus' command and carried on His ministry after His resurrection. "And they went forth, and preached every where, the Lord working with them, and confirming the word with signs following" (Mark 16:20).

It is true, that some people have brought undo attention to themselves, and may have even made a spectacle of praying for the sick, and have opened themselves, and the gospel of divine healing, to criticism. But, after all that, Jesus is still the Healer! If you are looking to the ability of man for your healing, you will not receive anything, but if you will look to the Lord, you can receive from the Lord.

Consider this: Jesus is the Savior. Preachers are not the Savior, are they? No, Jesus is the Savior. So when a person preaches that God will forgive sin, the media doesn't blast the news on radio and television, saying someone is claiming to be the Savior. Do they? And if one preaches that Jesus is the Healer, he is not making himself the Healer, anymore than he makes himself the Savior. Again, if one preaches that Jesus is the Deliverer from addictions and bondage, and emotional and mental distress, and trouble of any kind, that person is not claiming to be the deliverer himself. Jesus is the deliverer! He is the Savior, and He is the healer! And when one preaches that the Baptism of the Holy Ghost is still valid today, imparting power for victorious living, and accompanied by the evidence of speaking with other tongues, that doesn't mean he claims to be the one who baptizes with the Holy Ghost. Who is the baptizer with the Holy Ghost? Jesus Christ. "He will baptize you with the Holy Ghost and with fire" (Luke 3:16).

So, in all of this, we are simply presenting the message of the gospel of Jesus Christ.

Jesus is the One who forgives sin.
Jesus is the One who delivers from bondage.
Jesus is the One who heals,
Jesus is the One who baptizes in the Holy Ghost.

Review Questions
Chapter 9

HAS JESUS CHANGED?

1. Jesus Christ came to earth to "destroy the works of the devil" (I John 3:8). What works did Jesus do?

   (1)
   _____
   _____

   (2)
   _____
   _____

   (3)
   _____
   _____

   (4)
   _____
   _____

(5)

(6)

2. How does the purpose of Jesus relate to our lives as believers?

John 17:4

I John 4:17

JESUS IS THE HEALER

3. What two goals did Jesus Christ fulfill according to John 17:4 ?

1)_____

_____

2)_____

_____

4. How did Jesus fulfill these goals?   (John 17: 6-9)

(1)_____

_____

(2)_____

_____

(3)_____

_____

[SEE APPENDIX, "Names of God"]

3. What were the prayers Jesus offered for His disciples, that we should also pray?

   John 17: 11-24

   (1) _____
   _____

   (2) _____
   _____

   (3) _____
   _____

   (4) _____
   _____

   (5) _____
   _____

6. What prayer did Jesus pray four times in John 17? Why has it not fully been answered?

   _____
   _____
   _____
   _____

JESUS IS THE HEALER

7. How can we know miracles did not cease with the death of the Apostle John?

_____
_____
_____
_____
_____
_____
_____
_____

8. Jesus has not changed. He gave His disciples a Great Commission in Mark 16:15-18, and in it He told them to continue the work He had begun. The Great Commission includes:

(1)

(2)

9. He said these signs would follow *them that believe* (i.e., them that have FAITH):

    (1)

    (2)

    (3)

    (4)

    (5)

10. Some believe this commission was only for first century believers, but Jesus made it clear that His command was until the end of the age.

JESUS IS THE HEALER

Matthew :

    Begins with

_____
_____

    Ends with

_____
_____

Mark:

    Begins with

_____
_____

    Ends with

_____
_____

Luke:

    Begins with

_____
_____

    Ends with

_____
_____

John:

        Begins with _____

_____

        Ends with _____

_____

11. How do we know Jesus has not changed?

_____
_____
_____
_____
_____
_____
_____

12. What does the full gospel of Jesus Christ include?

_____
_____
_____
_____
_____

10

WHO CAN RECEIVE FROM GOD?

The prophet Isaiah asked this question, "to whom is the arm of the Lord revealed?" (Isaiah 53:1) King David asked, "Who shall ascend into the hill of the Lord? (into His presence) or who shall stand in His holy place? He that hath clean hands, and a pure heart; who hath not lifted up his soul unto vanity, nor sworn deceitfully. He shall receive the blessing from the Lord, and righteousness from the God of his salvation" (Psalm 24:3-5).

The person who can receive from God is one who comes humbly to God with childlike faith, trusting God for mercy, and believing to see God's goodness and power. King David said, "I had fainted (given up), unless I had believed to see the goodness of the Lord in the land of the living"
(Psalm 27:13).

In Psalm 103: 1-5, David said, "Bless the Lord, O my soul: and all that is within me, bless his holy name. Bless the Lord, O my soul, and forget not all his benefits: Who <u>forgiveth</u> all thine iniquites; who <u>healeth</u> all thy diseases: Who <u>redeemeth</u> thy life from destruction; who <u>crowneth</u> thee with loving kindness and tender mercies; Who <u>satisfieth</u> thy mouth with good thing; so that thy youth is renewed like the eagle's."

Five things in this passage the Lord does for man he created and loves. Numbers have meaning in the Bible, and the number "five" has significance here because it is the number of "grace" (God's undeserved favor and ability, made available to man). Has God's grace passed away?

If you say that God no longer heals today, how do you know He still forgives sin? The same Jesus who healed the sick when He walked on earth, is alive today, and will cure cancer, diabetes, high blood pressure, blindness, deafness, mental disease, drug addiction, alcoholism—Jesus is the answer! Now, what's the problem?

Jesus is alive and He is with us. He said, "Lo, I am with you always, even unto the end of the world" (Mt 28:19). Some believe He is here to forgive sin and give us a home in heaven, but they think He is far away from healing our bodies.

You Must Choose to Change Your Mind

Some people won't change their mind, and they won't change the subject. But we need to change both! Paul wrote in Romans 12:1-3 "present your bodies a living sacrifice, holy, acceptable unto God, which is your reasonable service, and be not conformed (molded) to this world: but be ye transformed by the renewing of your mind, that you may prove what is that good, and acceptable, and perfect, will of God."

1. Present your body to God. Change your mind from presenting your body to sin, and pleasure, and selfishness, to presenting your body to God, to live for Him and His eternal purpose for you.
2. Be not conformed to this world. Change your mind by choosing to mold yourself to God's ways.
3. Be transformed, or changed, from the inside out, by renewing your mind in the Word of God. The Apostle Paul told Timothy, "Study to show yourself approved unto God, a workman that needeth not to be ashamed, rightly dividing the word of truth" (II Timothy 2:15)

If you say, "Well, if I see things, then I will believe," you probably will not see anything from God, because you have the order all wrong. Jesus said in John 11:40, "Said I not unto thee, that, if thou wouldest believe, thou shouldest see the glory of God?" If we've got wrong thinking about healing, we need to change our mind and get our thinking straightened out.

Your Most Important Decision

The most important decision you will ever make in this life, and the most important question you will ever answer, is, "What will I do with Jesus?" The answer to this question determines your eternal destiny.

Salvation is God's eternal plan for man. But salvation includes more than forgiveness of sins, it also includes healing for our bodies. Without doubt, salvation is the most important decision, because <u>you can go to Heaven with sickness in your body, but you cannot go to Heaven with sin in your heart.</u>

Review Questions
Chapter 10

WHO CAN RECEIVE FROM GOD?

1. Who can receive from God? What qualities are necessary to receive?

   _____
   _____
   _____
   _____
   _____
   _____

2. How can we know healing (and all the promises of God) are for modern generations?

   _____
   _____
   _____
   _____

3. What five things does God promise His people in Psalm 103:1-5?

    1)

    2)

    3)

    4)

    5)

4. What is the significance of the number "Five" in scripture?

_____
_____
_____
_____
_____
_____
_____
_____

5. How can we change our mind toward God's promises, according to Romans 12:1-3?

    1)

    2)

6. What two things must change if we are to walk in divine healing and health?

   1)

   2)

7. How we can we find the perfect will of God for our lives?

8. What is the best time to believe for healing?

9. What is the correct order of behavior to see the glory of God?

10. What is the most important question you will answer in your life?

_____
_____
_____
_____

11. Why is this the most important question in life?

_____
_____
_____
_____

TERRY KINARD

11

WHY ARE SOME NOT HEALED?

Everyone <u>can</u> be healed, but
Not everyone <u>will</u> be healed.

Do we have to wait until we get to Heaven to be healed? No, we can be healed right now! God sent His Son, Jesus, to pay the redemptive price for sin and all that goes with it, including sickness, emotional distress, poverty...

God in His mercy, saw the condition of mankind and came to our rescue. God is real. His power is real. Equally real are the persons of the Godhead, the sacrifice of our Lord Jesus Christ on Calvary, and the completeness of the power of His shed blood to atone not only for our sins, but our sicknesses as well. Our standing before God to ask for His forgiveness and/or His healing is based on His love and His mercy and His sacrifice alone.

(1) Some Will Not Meet God's Requirements

Let me ask you a question: Will everyone be saved? The obvious answer is "No, not everyone will be saved." Can everyone by saved? Potentially, yes. Even though Jesus died to save the whole world, not everyone will be saved, because not everyone will hear the "good news," humble themselves, repent of their sin, and receive His salvation. But just because everyone will not be saved, why shouldn't you and I be saved? And in the same way, Jesus' suffering and death paid the price for divine, miraculous healing, but not everyone will humble themselves, repent of their sin, and receive His healing. One can be forgiven, and have a sure home in Heaven, and yet still not receive God's provision for healing. However, just because everyone will not be healed, why shouldn't you and I be healed?

(2) Healing is the Children's Bread

<u>Healing belongs to God's children</u>. You may say, "Must I repent to be healed? Yes, you must repent if you wish to receive healing by faith, because healing, like salvation, is called the "children's bread." (Matthew 15:26). Although God "is in the heavens, and does whatsoever pleases him" (   ), you may receive healing by His mercy as an "exceptional" event, if you are uncommitted and outside of the perimeters of His saving grace.

Healing was purchased for repentant, humble children of God, by the same precious blood of Jesus, for those who have asked God to forgive their sins, and have been "born again" into His family. <u>If you have asked Jesus Christ to forgive your sins and change your heart and save you, then healing belongs to you.</u> You can receive divine healing for your physical, emotional, and spiritual needs.

If you have not repented (turned away from) and asked God's forgiveness, you are merely "hoping" God may glance in your direction. It is a chance, a gamble, you do not have to take. Turn to God with all your heart, and enter into His privileged family today!

(3) Some Healing May Be Gradual

<u>Healing may require patience</u>. God meets people on the basis and level of their faith. Many times, He will begin a healing work to encourage a person to go deeper into God's love and grace, so faith can grow, and healing can be complete.

Gradual healing may even be a greater blessing, in that it presses us into greater depth in God. "Being confident of this very thing, that he which hath begun a good work in you will perform it until the day of Jesus Christ" (Philippians 1:6). The Lord wants us to continue to walk with Him, and grow "for precept must be upon precept, precept upon precept; line upon line, line upon line, here a little, and there a
little" (Isaiah 28:10). And Hosea wrote "then shall we know, if we follow on to know the Lord" (Hosea 6:3). If the Lord gave every healing instantly, we might take Him for granted, and walk away from Him.

It takes greater faith to receive instantaneous healing, and many are simply not built up in the Word enough to receive it. Some believe they deserve the sickness to some degree or other, and thus, they cannot receive instant healing.

We may have eternal life through Jesus Christ, God's only Son. He came to earth, lived a perfect life, and became our sacrifice for sin.

He took our penalty, and redeemed us from the curse, so we can go free! When we ask God to forgive our sin and be our Lord, we are "born again" or "saved." We receive the Lord Jesus as our Savior, and become a child of God, entitled to all His blessings, which includes healing

12

FAITH IS THE KEY TO HEALING

Faith sees the invisible;
believes the incredible;
receives the impossible.

"For without faith it is impossible to please God; for he that cometh to God must believe that He is, and that He is a rewarder of them who diligently seek Him." Hebrews 11:6.

<u>God's will is for each one of us to live life to its fullest, be free from sickness and disease, and fulfill the number of our days</u>. Some of you reading this do not believe this statement, for immediately you are filled with painful memories of those you love, who were not healed, although prayer was made and many tears were shed.

There are many reasons why people are not successful in appropriating their healing and we will explore many of them. We will also explore the basis in God's Word of the doctrine of Divine Healing, and explain the scriptures, so that you may forever settle in your mind God's good will for your life. He came that we might have abundant life (John 10:10). But until we understand what the will of the Lord is, we are building our spiritual house on the sand, and it may not withstand the storms of sickness and disease that the devil would stir up against us.

TERRY KINARD

"Success occurs when opportunity meets preparation."

"Wherefore be ye not unwise, but understanding what the will of the Lord is" (Ephesians 5:17).

Pray as you read and study God's Word through this book. Remember, His promises reveal what He wants to do for us, but <u>can only do when we stand in faith.</u> We pray for you also,

"That the God of our Lord Jesus Christ, the Father of glory, may give unto you the spirit of wisdom and revelation in the knowledge of him: The eyes of your understanding being enlightened; that ye may know what is the hope of his calling, and what the riches of the glory of his inheritance in the saints, and what is the exceeding greatness of his power to usward who believe, according to the working of his mighty power..." (Ephesians 1:17-19).

As we sincerely and honestly approach God's Word concerning His Will in this physical area of divine healing, let us "search the scriptures...(for Jesus said) they are they which testify of me" (John 5:39). Jesus also said, "the words that I speak unto you, they are spirit and they are life" (John 6:63). He said, "...attend unto my words...keep them in the midst of thine heart...for they are <u>life</u> to those that find them, and <u>health</u> to all their flesh" (Proverbs 4:22).

Do you, or someone you care about, suffer with pain? Do you need the healing touch of Jesus in your body? Are you upset, depressed, oppressed, addicted, overwhelmed? Have you felt helpless, and unable to take control of physical calamities that unmercifully pound your life like hurricane-driven waves upon the seashore?

There is help! There is hope! God is your answer! There is power over "all the power of the enemy." God is able to do "...exceeding abundantly above all we can ask or think, according to the power that worketh in us" (Ephesians 3:20).

Let me encourage you to carefully attend to His Words and the simple truth that God has provided for our well-being, spirit, soul, and _body_. Unbelief is sin, because the Word tells us "whatsoever is not of faith is sin" (Romans 14:23). Follow the example of King David of old, who testified, "Thy Word have I hid in my heart, that I might not sin against thee" (Psalm 119:11).

Remember, doubt is the opposite of faith, and "without faith, it is impossible to please God" (Hebrews 11:6). "If thou canst believe, all things are possible to him that believes" (Mark 9:23).

How You Can Believe

How can you move from unbelief to faith?
How can you pass from the sadness of disappointment and fear into the gladness of assurance in the full provision of God?

There is only one way to truth.
There is only one path to peace.
There is only one refuge of comfort.
There is only one source of power.
That way,
That path,
That refuge,
That source, is Jesus Christ.

We come to the Father through Jesus Christ. "Jesus saith, I am the way, the truth, and the life: no man cometh unto the Father, but by me" (John 14:6). He said, "And ye shall seek me, and find me, when ye shall search for me with all your heart. And I will be found of you, saith the Lord..." (Jeremiah 29:13,14).

We come to Jesus through faith (a right reaction to His ability). "But without faith it is impossible to please him: for he that cometh to God must believe that he is, and that he is a rewarder of them that diligently seek him" (Hebrews 11:6). "..So then faith cometh

(is set in place) by hearing, and hearing by the word (rhema) of God"
(Romans 10:17).

Without faith in God's ability, one cannot receive healing, or any other good thing, from His storehouse of "exceeding abundantly above all we can ask or think…"
(Ephesians 3:20).

The promise is "according to the power that worketh in us," and this power comes from faith. According to Romans 10:17, this right reaction, or faith, comes from hearing the "word" of God. In the Greek (which is the original language of the New Testament) "word" in Romans 10:17 is originally the Greek word "rhema." So then the verse would read "...so then faith cometh by hearing, and hearing by the "rhema" of God."

How can you know that God is "able" to heal, and yet not receive your healing? You cannot receive healing without a quickening of God's Word to your human mind and spirit. Faith comes through a "rhema" word, a "spirit-breathed" word to your heart and understanding.

> "Rhema" is a word from God that is quickened, or made alive, by the Spirit of God. To say it another way, when we read a promise from God's Word, it is merely words on paper, "letter" or "logos." It will not become effective in our lives until it has been breathed upon by the Holy Spirit of God. When God breathes on His word, it becomes "Rhema" or Spirit-quickened, to us. "...for the letter (logos) kills, but the spirit gives life" (II Corinthians 3:6).

Chapter 12
Review Questions

Faith is the Key to Healing

1. What is God's will for each one of us?

2. What scriptures tell us that God desires us to have abundant life?

3. What scriptures tell us that God desires us to be free from sickness and disease?

4. What scriptures tell us that God desires us to live long and fulfill our days?

JESUS IS THE HEALER

5. How can we withstand the storms of life, including sickness and disease?

6. How can we build our spiritual house upon the Rock?

7. The promises of God reveal

8. God can only fulfill His promises for us

_____
_____
_____
_____
_____
_____
_____

9. What is the way to divine health?

_____
_____
_____
_____
_____

10. What is the power that works in us?

_____
_____
_____
_____
_____
_____
_____
_____

JESUS IS THE HEALER

11. There is only one _____ to truth,

12. There is only one _____ to peace

13. There is only one _____ of comfort, _____

_____
_____
_____
_____
_____
_____
_____

14. There is only one _____ of power,

_____
_____
_____
_____
_____

15. How do we approach God the Father?

_____
_____
_____
_____
_____
_____
_____
_____

16. How do we approach Jesus Christ?

_____
_____
_____
_____
_____

17. What is faith?

_____
_____
_____
_____
_____

18. The promise of faith is according to

_____
_____
_____
_____
_____
_____
_____
_____

19. The Greek word "rhema" means

___

20. The Greek word "logos," means

___

21. What limits our faith?

___

13

HOW TO RECEIVE HEALING

Although some of the following concepts overlap the previous chapter on "Why Some are Not Healed," I thought it was important to set down in a condensed format a checklist for anyone who is seeking God for healing. Exercise yourself by using your faith to receive healing for small infirmities, such as headache, eye strain, sore muscles, etc. It is much the same as weight lifting, and is much easier to accomplish by starting out gradually and building strength for greater faith. As you grow in God, your faith will get stronger and stronger, to resist the devil on your own.

"These signs shall follow them that believe...they shall lay hands on the sick, and they shall recover" (Mark 16:17-18). <u>You can lay hands on yourself, and pray, and receive healing by faith.</u> You can lay hands on others who are sick, and see them healed also. Jesus gave all true believers authority, through faith in His name, to pray for the sick to be healed. There are times in all of our lives, however, when we need to receive the "effectual fervent prayer of a righteous man that availeth much" (James 5:16). And for that reason these instructions are offered as a guide for receiving your healing.

Divine healing is the manifestation of the power of God in the lives of men, overcoming physical afflictions in a supernatural way. Divine healing is an act of God, not based upon the power of man's intellect, mental suggestion, or physical therapy.

Smith Wigglesworth, one of the great giants of faith, said of prayer for healing, "Opportunity does not wait, not even while we pray. We must live ready." Someone once said, "Success occurs when opportunity meets preparation." It is true in all areas of spiritual life, and especially healing. Check yourself by these guidelines, and enjoy the health, joy and peace that are in Christ Jesus!

Prayer for Healing By Elders

"Is any sick among you? Let him <u>call for the elders of the church</u>; and <u>let them pray over him, anointing him with oil in the name of the Lord</u>: And the <u>prayer of faith shall save the sick</u>, and <u>the Lord shall raise him up</u>; and <u>if he have committed sins, they shall be forgiven him</u>. <u>Confess your faults</u> one to another, and <u>pray one for another</u>, that ye may be healed. The <u>effectual fervent prayer of a righteous man availeth much</u>" (James 5:14-16).

This is the Biblical pattern for receiving healing by the laying on of hands by the elders of the church:

1. **<u>Call for the elders of your church</u>**. (v 14)Your spiritual leaders should be willing to come to you and pray, if you are unable to get to them. If you are attending a church whose elders do not believe in healing through faith in the Lord Jesus,

leave immediately, and find a good Bible-believing, God-honoring church.

2. **The elders should anoint you with oil as they pray in the name of the Lord Jesus for your healing.** (v 14) Oil is a symbol of the Holy Spirit, and He is the agent through which we receive God's blessings. Having your church elders (pastors) anoint you with oil when they pray for your healing, is a recognizing of the unseen presence of the Holy Spirit, and a sign of consecration, or submission to God, on your part.

3. **The prayer of "faith" shall save the sick.** (v 15) Follow leaders of faith and integrity, so you can respect them and love them and have confidence in their level of faith. Peace will follow, and you will receive healing when they pray. (If you do not respect your leaders as men and women of God, you may not receive your healing by their prayers.) "Know them which labor among you, and are over you in the Lord, and admonish you...esteem them very highly in love for their work's sake. And be at peace among yourselves" (I Thessalonians 5:12). <u>If you are not in peace, you are not in faith</u>, for "faith worketh by love" (Ga 5:6). **The Lord shall raise him up.** (v 15) God's will, done God's way, always brings God's results. When we follow God's commandments, we can be confident of positive results.

4 <u>**And if you have committed sins, they will be forgiven...confess your faults...and pray...that ye may be healed.**</u> If you are afflicted, you must be willing to confess any

sins you may have committed, in order to be healed. (vv 15-16) Jesus died both to forgive sin and heal sickness. "He that covereth his sins shall not prosper: but whoso confesseth and forsaketh them shall have mercy" (Proverbs 28:13). The statement "the Lord shall raise him up" indicates immediate or quick healing may be expected.

These simple steps will produce Bible results of divine healing, <u>if we are personally prepared to receive the prayer of faith</u>. "They that observe lying vanities forsake their own mercy" (Jonah 2:8). We must be honest with God and with ourselves, and take the necessary steps to insure we are ready to receive our healing. "Examine yourselves, whether ye be in the faith; prove your own selves" (II Corinthians 13:5).

Review Chapter 13

1. How should we "exercise" our faith for healing?

We exercise our faith by believing for minor ailments to be healed, much like exercising our physical bodies through weight lifting.

2. Why should we lay hands on ourself for healing?

There is healing in our hands by the promise of God. "These signs shall follow them that believe...they shall lay hands on the sick, and they shall recover" (Mark 16:17-18).

3. When should we call the elders of the church to come to us and pray for healing?

We should call for the elders of the church if we are unable to come to them for prayer.

4. What should we look for in spiritual elders, or leaders?

We must follow men and women of integrity, who have a living relationship with God, and who walk in high levels of faith. Whomever we submit to as leaders are our spiritual covering, and will pray over us when we need healing on a level we cannot reach on our own. The faith of our leaders is life or death to us.

5. When should you submit to leadership who do not believe in the healing power of God, and who are not willing to anoint and pray for the sick according to James 5:13-16?

Never.

6. According to James 5:15, what must the afflicted person do to receive healing?

> Anyone afflicted who wishes to be anointed with oil, and prayed over by elders, must confess any known sin in his or her life, if they expect to receive healing.

TERRY KINARD

14

Guidelines for Those Who Need Healing

The following guidelines should be followed <u>before</u> you call for the elders of the church. They will prepare you to receive your healing, when you are anointed according to God's Word in James 5:13-16.

1. Be Sure You are in Right Standing with God.

Make sure you have no known sin in your heart. "He that covereth his sins shall not prosper: but whoso confesseth and forsaketh them shall have mercy" (Proverbs 28:13). Remember, you can go to Heaven with sickness in your body, but you cannot go to Heaven with sin in your heart. "Who can understand his errors? Cleanse thou me from secret faults. Keep back thy servant also from presumptuous sins..." (Psalm 19:12-13). "The heart is deceitful above all things, and desperately wicked: who can know it? I the Lord search the heart, I try the reins, even to give every man according to his ways, and according to the fruit of his doings" (Jeremiah 17:9-10).

<u>Salvation for our spirit is more important than healing for our body</u>. Confess your sin to Him, and ask forgiveness. "If we confess our sins, he is faithful and just to forgive us our sins, and to cleanse us from all unrighteousness" (I John 1:9). Healing is the "children's bread" (Matthew 15:26). It belongs to those who are forgiven, and look to Jesus as Lord.

2. Be at peace with all men as much as is within your power to do so.

Keep stress and strife out of your relationships at all costs. Pride is the root of most, if not all, strife, and must be uncovered and dealt with. "the servant of the Lord must not strive; but be gentle unto all men…" (II Timothy 2:24). "If it be possible, as much as lieth in you, live peaceably with all men" (Romans 12:18). "Therefore if thou bring thy gift to the altar, and there remember that thy brother hath aught against thee; leave there thy gift before the altar…first be reconciled…and then come…" (Matthew 5:23). "And when ye stand praying, forgive, if ye have aught against any: that your Father also which is in heaven may forgive you your trespasses" (Mark 11:25). "A sound heart is the life of the flesh: but envy the rottenness of the bones" (Proverbs 14:30). If we have problems in relationships, it is very difficult to receive healing.

3. Build up yourself in true faith by studying God's Word.

"Let us therefore come boldly unto the throne of grace, that we may obtain mercy, and find grace to help in time of need" (Hebrews 4:16). "My son, attend to my words; incline thine ear unto my sayings. Let them not depart from thine eyes; keep them in the midst of thine heart. For they (words of godly wisdom) are life to those that find them, and health to all their flesh" (Proverbs 4:20-22). "So then faith cometh by hearing, and hearing by the word of God" (Romans 10:17).

4. Apply your heart to meditate and understand the sufferings of Christ.

"The natural man receiveth not the things of the Spirit of God: for they are foolishness unto him: neither can he know them, because they are spiritually discerned:"(I Corinthians 2:14). "I will meditate also of all thy work, and talk of thy doings" (Psalm 77:12).

We should meditate on the Lord until the truth gets down in our spirit, not merely in our mind. We do not have to be sick. "Let the words of my mouth, and the meditation of my heart, be acceptable in thy sight, O Lord, my strength, and my redeemer" (Psalm 19:14). "the meditation of my heart shall be of understanding" (Psalm 49:3b). "Himself took our infirmities and bare our sicknesses" (Matthew 8:17).

5. Testify and declare the goodness and mercy and powerful works of God.

"Let no corrupt communication proceed out of your mouth, but that which is good to the use of edifying, that it may minister grace unto the hearers. And grieve not the Holy Spirit of God, whereby ye are sealed
unto the day of redemption" (Ephesians 4:29-30). "My mouth shall speak of wisdom" (Psalm 49:3). "Whoso offereth praise glorifieth me: and to him that ordereth his conversation aright will I show the salvation of God" (Psalm 50:23).

6. Sanctify (set apart) yourself fully to Christ.

"Present your bodies a living sacrifice, holy, acceptable unto god, which is your reasonable service. And be not conformed to this world: but be ye transformed by the renewing of your mind, that ye may prove what is that good, and acceptable, and perfect, will of God" (Romans 12:1-2).

7. Choose friends with high levels of faith.

"Be not deceived: evil communications corrupt good manners" (I Corinthians 15:33). "Should you help the ungodly, and love them that hate the Lord? Therefore is wrath upon thee from before the Lord" (II Chronicles 19:2). "He that walketh with wise men shall be wise: but a companion of fools shall be destroyed" (Proverbs 13:20).

8. Live in Praise and Worship Before You See the Answer.

Pray every day, and be thankful for God's blessings. "Continue in prayer, and watch in the same with thanksgiving" (Colossians 4:2). Be thankful to God regardless of your circumstance, recognizing His greatness. Then you will have faith, or confidence, to ask His help during times of trial and testing. "Offer unto God thanksgiving; and pay thy vows unto the most High: And call upon me in the day of trouble: I will deliver thee, and thou shalt glorify me" (Psalm 50:14-15). "Rejoice in the Lord always: and again I say, Rejoice...be careful for nothing; but in everything by prayer and supplication with thanksgiving let your requests be made known unto God" (Philippians 4:4,6).

"Serve the Lord with gladness: come before his presence with singing..." (Psalm 100:2). "I will bless the Lord at all times: his praise shall continually be in my mouth" (Psalm 34:1).

9. Resist the Devil.

"Submit yourselves therefore to God, Resist the devil, and he will flee from you" (James 4:7) "Be sober, be vigilant; because your adversary the devil, as a roaring lion, walketh about, seeking whom he may devour: whom resist steadfast in the faith..."
(I Peter 5:8-9).

10. Press into God for Divine Health while you are well.

> "But ye, beloved, building up yourselves on your most holy faith, praying in the Holy Ghost, Keep yourselves

in the love of God, looking for the mercy of our Lord Jesus Christ unto eternal life" (Jude 20-21). "Wherefore take unto you the whole armor of God, that ye may be able to withstand in the evil day, and having done all, to stand. Stand therefore..." (Ephesians 6:13)

TERRY KINARD

15

HEALING SCRIPTURES

1.
Obey God and Be Healed.
Exodus 15:26

If thou wilt diligently hearken (listen) to the voice of the Lord thy God, and wilt do that which is right in his sight, and wilt give ear to his commandments, and keep all his statutes, I will put none of these diseases upon thee, which I have brought upon the Egyptians: for I am the Lord that healeth thee.

2.
Serve God and Experience Healing
Exodus 23:25

And ye shall serve the Lord your God, and he shall bless thy bread, and thy water; and I will take sickness away from the midst of thee...the number of thy days I will fulfill.

3.
Honor God and He'll take Sickness Away From You
Deuteronomy 7:15

And the Lord will take away from thee all sickness, and will put one of the evil diseases of Egypt, which thou knowest, upon thee; but will lay them upon all them that hate thee.

4.
Choose to live! Fight for your life!
Deuteronomy 30:19

But if thine heart turn away, so that thou wilt not hear, but shalt be drawn away, and worship other gods, and serve them; I denounce unto you this day, that ye shall surely perish, and that ye shall not prolong your days upon the land, whither thou passest over Jordan to go to possess it. <u>I call heaven and earth to record this day against you, that I have set before you life and death, blessing and cursing: therefore choose life, that both thou and thy seed may live:</u> That thou mayest love the Lord thy God, and that thou mayest obey his voice, and that thou mayest cleave unto him: for he is thy life, and the length of thy days: that thou mayest dwell in the land which the Lord sware unto thy fathers, to Abraham, to Isaac, and to Jacob, to give them.

5.
God's Word will not Fail.
Joshua 21:45

There failed not ought of any good thing which the Lord had spoken unto the house of Israel; all came to pass.

6.
Set Your Love Upon God, and
Live a Long Life
Psalm 91:14-16

Because he hath set his love upon me, therefore will I deliver him: I will set him on high, because he hath known my name. He shall call upon me, and I will answer him: I will be with him in trouble;

I will deliver him, and honour him. <u>With long life will I satisfy him, and show him my salvation.</u>

7.
Healing is One of God's Great Benefits.
Psalm 103:1-5

Bless the Lord, O my soul: and all that is within me, bless his holy name. Bless the Lord, O my soul, and forget not all his benefits: <u>Who forgiveth all thine iniquities; who healeth all thy diseases;</u> Who redeemeth thy life from destruction; who crowneth thee with lovingkindness and tender mercies; who satisfieth thy mouth with good things; so that thy youth is renewed like the eagle's.

8.
God's Word is a Healing Word
Psalm 107:20

He sent His Word and healed them, and delivered them from their destructions.

9.
God Wants You to Live
Psalm 118:17

I shall not die, but live, and declare the works of the Lord.

10.
Know God's Word. It will save your life.
Proverbs 4:20-23

My son, attend to my words; incline thine ear unto my sayings. Let them not depart from thine eyes; keep them in the midst of thine heart. <u>For they are life unto those that find them, and health to all their flesh.</u>

11.
Plead Your Case to God
Isaiah 43:25-26

I, even I, am he that blotteth out thy transgressions for mine own sake, and will not remember thy sins. Put me in remembrance: let us plead together: declare thou, that thou mayest be justified.

12.
Jesus Redeemed Us From
Sin and Sickness
Isaiah 53:4-5

Surely he hath borne our griefs (sicknesses), and carried our sorrows (pains)... But he was wounded for our transgressions, he was bruised for our iniquities: the chastisement of our peace was upon him; and <u>with his stripes we are healed.</u>

13.
God will Restore Health to You.
Jeremiah 30:17

For I will restore health unto thee, and I will heal thee of thy wounds, saith the Lord; because they called thee an Outcast, saying, This is Zion, whom no man seeketh after..

14.
God's Word tell us to Declare Strength
Joel 3:10

Let the weak say, "I am strong."

15.
Sickness will not Come Back
Nahum 1:9

What do ye imagine against the Lord? He will make an utter end: affliction shall not rise up the second time.

16.
Pay All Your Tithes, and Receive
All God's Blessings.
Malachi 3:8-11

Will a man rob God? Yet ye have robbed me But ye say, Wherein have we robbed thee? In tithes and offerings. Ye are cursed with a curse: for ye have robbed me, even this whole nation. Bring ye all the tithes into the storehouse, that there may be meat in mine house, and prove me now herewith, saith the Lord of hosts, if I will not open you the windows of heaven, and pour you out a blessing, that there shall not be room enough to receive it. And I will rebuke the devourer for your sakes…

17.
It Is God's Will
For You To Be Healed
Matthew 8:1-3

When he was come down from the mountain, great multitudes followed him. And, behold, there came a leper and worshipped him, saying, Lord, if thou wilt, thou canst make me clean. And Jesus put forth his hand, and touched him, saying, I will; be thou clean. And immediately his leprosy was cleansed.

18.
You Can Take Authority Over
Sickness In Your Body
Matthew 18:18

Verily I say unto you, Whatsoever ye shall bind on earth shall be bound in heaven; and whatsoever ye shall loose on earth shall be loosed in heaven.

19.
Pray in Agreement with Someone
For Your Healing
Matthew 18:19

Again I say unto you, That if two of you shall agree on earth as touching any thing that they shall ask, it shall be done for them of my Father which is in heaven.

20.
What You Say Will Make a Difference
Mark 11:22-23

And Jesus answering saith unto them, Have faith in God. For verily I say unto you, That whosoever shall say unto this mountain, Be thou removed, and be thou cast into the sea; and shall not doubt in his heart, but shall believe that those things which he saith shall come to pass; he shall have whatsoever he saith.

21.
Believe God, and You Will Receive
Mark 11:24

Therefore I say unto you, What things soever ye desire, when ye pray, believe that ye receive them, and ye shall have them...and when ye stand praying, forgive...

22.
Have Someone Lay Their Hand Upon You and Pray for Healing
Mark 16:17,18

And these signs shall follow them that believe; In my name . . .They will lay hands on the sick, and they will recover.

23.
Be a Worshipper of God.
John 9:31

Now we know that God heareth not sinners: but if any man be a worshipper of God, and doeth his will, him he heareth.

24.
The Devil Wants to Kill You; God Wants to Heal You
John 10:10

The thief cometh not, but for to steal, and to kill, and to destroy: I am come that they might have life, and that they might have it more abundantly.

25.
The Spirit of God gives Life.
Romans 8:11

But if the Spirit of him that raised up Jesus from the dead dwell in you, he that raised up Christ from the dead shall also quicken your mortal bodies by his Spirit that dwelleth in you...If ye live after the flesh, ye shall die: but if ye through the Spirit do mortify the deeds of the body, ye shall live

26.
God's Promises Are True
II Corinthians 1:20

For all the promises of God in him are yea, and in him Amen, unto the glory of God by us.

27.
Our Faith is Mighty Through God
II Corinthians 10:4-5

For the weapons of our warfare Are not carnal, but mighty through God to the pulling down of strong holds; Casting down imaginations, and every high thing that exalteth itself against the knowledge of God, and bringing into captivity every thought to the obedience of Christ.

28.
Christ Redeemed Us From Sin and
Sickness, the Curse of the Law
Galatians 3:13

Christ hath redeemed us from the curse of the law, being made a curse for us: for it is written, Cursed is every one that hangeth on a tree...that we might receive the promise of the Spirit through faith.

29.
Put on God's Armor.
Fight for Your Healing
Ephesians 6:10-15

Finally, my brethren, be strong in the Lord, and in the power of his might. Put on the whole armor of God, that ye may be able to stand against the wiles of the devil. For we wrestle not against flesh and blood, but against principalities, against powers, against the rulers of the darkness of this world, against spiritual wickedness in high places. Wherefore take unto you the whole armor of God, that ye may be able to withstand in the evil day, and having done all, to stand.Stand therefore, having your loins girt about with truth and having on the breast plate of righteousness; and your feet shod with the preparation of the gospel of peace;

30.
The Most Important Armor, Faith
Ephesians 6:16-18

Above all, taking the shield of faith, wherewith ye shall be able to quench all the fiery darts of the wicked And take the helmet of salvation, and the sword of the Spirit, which is the word of God: Praying always with all prayer and supplication in the Spirit, and watching thereunto with all perseverance and supplication for all saints.

31.
Healing is God's Will.
It is Working In You.
Philippians 2:12-13

...work out your own salvation With fear and trembling. For it is God which worketh in you both to will and to do of his good pleasure.

32.
Fear is Not of God. Rebuke it!
II Timothy 1:7

For God hath not given us the spirit of fear; but of power, and of love, and of a sound mind.

33.
Do Not Waver In Your Faith.
Hebrews 10:23

Let us hold fast the profession of our faith without wavering; (for he is faithful that promised)

34.
Hold on To Your Faith With Patience
Hebrews 10:35

Cast not away therefore your confidence, which hath great recompense of reward.For ye have need of patience, that, after ye have done the will of God, ye might receive the promise.

35.
Jesus Christ does not Change.
What He did in the Bible,
He will do for you.
Hebrews 13:8

Jesus Christ the same yesterday, and to day, and for ever.

36.
Have a Christian Leader
Who Believes In Healing
Anoint You with Oil and Pray
James 5:14-15

Is any sick among you? Let him call for the elders of the church; and let them pray over him, anointing him with oil in the name of the Lord: and the prayer of faith shall save the sick, and the Lord shall raise him up: and if he hath committed sins, they shall be forgiven him.

37.
Confess Your Faults
James 5:16

Confess your faults one to another, and pray one for another, that ye may be healed. The effectual fervent prayer of a righteous man availed much.

38.
Jesus Bought Your Healing
I Peter 2:24

Who his own self bare our sins in his own body on the tree, that we, being dead to sins, should live unto righteousness: by whose stripes ye were healed.

39.
Keep Your Heart Pure When You Pray
I John 3:20-22

For is our heart condemn us, God is greater than heart, and knoweth all things.Beloved, if our heart condemn us not, then have we confidence toward God. And whatsoever we ask, we receive of him, because we keep his commandments, and do those things that are pleasing in his sight.

40.
Be Confident When You Pray
I John 5:14-15

And this is the confidence that we have in him, that, if we ask any thing According to His will, he heareth us: And if we know that he hear us, whatsoever we ask, we know that we have the petitions that we desired of him.

41.
God Wants You to Be Well and Prosper
III John 2

Beloved, I wish above all things that thou mayest prosper and be in health, even as thy soul prospereth.

42.
Expect Healing from God.
Psalm 62:5

My soul, wait thou only upon God; for my expectation is from him.

43.
Testify About Your Healing
Revelation 12:11

And they overcame him by the blood of the Lamb, and by the word of their testimony; and they loved not their lives unto the death.

JESUS IS THE HEALER

THANK YOU!

We would love to hear from you,
if this book has been a blessing.
Contact us today, and consider sowing a
Financial seed to help us expand
our outreach.

Call or write us at:

HIGH CALL INTERNATIONAL
P.O.BOX 70
FATE,TX 75132

214-683-6207

Email: ttkinard@gmail.com

Visit us online at:
www.terrykinard.org

PERSONAL PRAYER PAGES

PERSONAL PRAYER PAGES

PERSONAL PRAYER PAGES

PERSONAL PRAYER PAGES

PERSONAL PRAYER PAGES

THANK YOU!

We would love to hear from you,
if this book has been a blessing.
Contact us today, and consider sowing a
Financial seed to help us expand
our outreach.

Call or write us at:

HIGH CALL INTERNATIONAL
P.O.BOX 70
FATE,TX 75132

214-683-6207

Email: ttkinard@gmail.com

Visit us online at:
www.terrykinard.org

JESUS IS THE HEALER

TERRY KINARD

www.ingramcontent.com/pod-product-compliance
Lightning Source LLC
Chambersburg PA
CBHW052058110526
44591CB00013B/2267